Headin' for the Sweet Heat

Fruit and Fire-Spice Cooking

Jacqueline Landeen

Illustrated by Michael Haswood

GIBBS·SMITH
→P
PUBLISHER

Salt Lake City

First Edition
99 98 97 96   10 9 8 7 6 5 4 3 2 1

This is a Peregrine Smith Book, published by
Gibbs Smith, Publisher
P.O. Box 667
Layton, Utah 84041

Book design and composition by
Kinara Graphics, Inc., Ogden, Utah - (801) 399-1932

Book edited by Caroll Shreeve
Printed and bound in Korea

Library of Congress Cataloging-in-Publication Data

Landeen, Jacqueline.
     Headin' for the sweet heat : fruit and fire-spice cooking /
Jacqueline Landeen : illustrations by Michael Haswood. — 1st ed.
          p.   cm.
     Includes index.
     ISBN 0-87905-759-9
     1. Cookery (Hot peppers) 2. Cookery (Fruit)   I. Title
TX803.P46L36 1996   96—15467
641.6'384—dc20   CIP

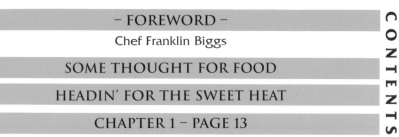

– FOREWORD –
Chef Franklin Biggs

SOME THOUGHT FOR FOOD

HEADIN' FOR THE SWEET HEAT

CHAPTER 1 – PAGE 13
Fruited Fiery Broths:
A Different Cooking Consideration
How Fruit and Fire-Spice Stocks Evolved
Varieties of Fruit and Fire-Spice Mother Stocks

CHAPTER 2 – PAGE 21
Fruited Fire in the Kitchen

CHAPTER 3 – PAGE 31
Leeks, Limes, Lilies:
Fruited Vinaigrettes

CHAPTER 4 – PAGE 38
No Stranger to Sweat:
Fruit-Fire Mustards

CHAPTER 5 – PAGE 46
High-Peasant Eats:
Appetizers

CHAPTER 6 – PAGE 53
Garden in a Pot:
Soups and Stews

CHAPTER 7 – PAGE 61
Tongue Touchers:
Enraged Suppers and Otherwise

CHAPTER 8 – PAGE 73
Sneakers and Gewürztraminer:
Solitary Meals

CHAPTER 9 – PAGE 81
Beginnings or Endings:
Sweet Dreams

CHAPTER 10 – PAGE 92
Innocent Pleasures in the Hidden West

BIBLIOGRAPHY – PAGE 93
INDEX – PAGE 94

FOREWORD

Life is an ever-evolving series of taste memories . . . layers upon layers which swirl and combine to evoke awareness of other senses, passions, and people. To speak of Jacqueline is to speak of passion, food, zest for living. Few people I know can take a food concept and develop it, describe it, communicate the passion for it so infectiously. It has been my pleasure to enjoy developing just such taste memories with Jacqueline. Our times together have always been centered around food, but never limited to just that intense interest. From the time I first met her, peering out of the kitchen-door windows of her bistro, JazRanch, as she wondered, "Who is that guy who is ordering EVERYTHING on the menu?; I have . . .you are in for a great treat. From a café au lait and hot baguette at Cafe Fanny in Berkeley, California, or a lamb al pesto at Cafe Mariposa in Deer Valley, Utah, to the numerous meals I enjoyed at her bistro. And always we would talk of people, food, places we'd been, places we were going . . . and always I am wondering what she is up to, where she is wandering, who she is getting excited about good food. I am touched with her love for that food, for the people who produce it, for the patrons who enjoy it. Her passion for life is intense, her love for good food is unlimited, her desire for an artful life is deep. If you, the reader of *Headin' for the Sweet Heat*, enjoy Jacqueline's food only half of what I do, you are in for a great treat. Prepare yourself to enjoy her way of looking at life and at food, developing new taste memories and passions. She is very special to me. **–Chef Franklin Biggs**

Franklin Biggs has a Grande Diplome from La Varenne Paris and a B.A. in political science from the University of California, Berkeley. His culinary travels have taken him from being a stagiaire at Taillevent, Maxim's and Patisserie Jean Millet in Paris to Executive Chef at Deer Valley Resort, Utah, The Lodge at Pebble Beach, California, The Claremont Resort and Spa in Berkeley, California, and The Buttes Resort in Tempe, Arizona. He is presently developing Jimmy's at Brookwood, a diner for the twenty-first century, in Birmingham, Alabama, where he lives with his wife, Susan Sell, an assistant professor of molecular genetics.

Grub First, Then Ethics
–Bertolt Brecht

ACKNOWLEDGEMENTS

To all past JazRanch patrons who remained loyal through the culinary experimental years:

Maestro Maurice Abravanel, Arthur Adelmann, Don Austin, Becky & Phil Bamberger, Peggy Battin, Franklin Biggs, L. 'Rusty' Brown, Brett Clifford, Debra & Peter Cole, Marilyn & Almon Covey, Company of Four, Peter Coyote, Susan & Joe Culbertson, Ro and Jim Dale, Dr. Bill DeVries, Dr. Hank Duffy, Marco Fowler, Professor Larry Gerlach, Tamara Gibo, Steven Goldsmith, Brooke Hopkins, The Howas—Joe, Rick, Tom, KSL, KUER, Dr. Robert Lynch, Jazz Man Fred McCray, Bill Nassikas, Gerry & Travis Nichols, Ricklen Nobis, Jackie Nokes, the Nords, Janet Robeson Olch, Jeff Polychronis, Riki Rafner, David & Cita Riley, Carol von Schmidt, Susan Sell, Bernardo Flores-Sahagun, David Shire, Mark & Jules Strand, Beanie & Steve Strasser, Leigh vonder Esch, Steve Williams, John Wilson, Steven Wood, the phantom lawyer who flew from Moab to Salt Lake City routinely for his lunch adventure, and to the rest of the JazRanch family of patrons . . . you were the quintessential Chicago audience . . . alive, spontaneous, and eager to enjoy the fruits of my labor.

To all past, present, knowing and unknowing supporters and inspirers:

Ray Atencio, Thomas Berry, Sue & Orion Bishop, Hiddenwest Cafe Troupe in Park City, Utah, Wes Bowen, Judith Borelli Caldwell, Lachlan Cooke, Bill Frazier, Sifu Jerry Gardiner, Chris Griscom—the Light Institute of Galisteio, New Mexico, Derek Haffar, The Haswoods, Frankie Kiesel, Kathleen and Donald Macdonald, Penelope & Dan McKay, Trompe l'oeil Man Chuck 'Bo' Nitti, Rita di Mario and her famiglia of Orvieto, Italy, Rachel Puccio, Chagdud Tulku Rinpoche, Megan Rosch, Gerri Azzaro Sambel, Carm & Nancy Santoro, Sammie Scaccia, Lisa Scharetg, Screenwriters' Guild of America West, St. Helena Napa Valley, California/Park City, Utah Connection, Sundance Institute, Vicki & Ted Walton, and the very special and enthusiastic staff at Peregrine Smith Books who are what all publishers should be, dreamweavers. To my editor Caroll Shreeve, for helping make this book exactly what I wanted it to be. She is this author's ultimate dream team. Thank you Gibbs & Cathy Smith for believing in *Headin' for the Sweet Heat* way back when and taking the chance to blaze the trail with me now in the Hidden West. To Jim and Harry, the last of the gentlemen cowboys, who made the dream a reality, you taught me never to look back, 'cause they might be gainin' on me. Happy Trails.

In memory of Genevieve and Santo,
and for Black Bart

SOME THOUGHT FOR FOOD

... that's what kept me going for so long in spite of everything,
the mystery, like the taste of a really good meal,
like a deep friendship, I love it.
–Rip Torn

Growing up Sicilian in Chicago tenaciously reinforced my childhood notion of what, how, why, and where I would cook as I do. Powerful is my memory of acting the coveted role of the Virgin Mary on St. Joseph's Day before an altar table spilling with endless fruit, vegetable, and seafood varieties. Whether it was a humble artichoke chile frittata or curiously fried orange-garlic-fennel octopus, the food was blessed and offered to St. Joseph on his annual feast day of March 19—the day when the swallows would or would not return to San Juan Capistrano. No visitors nor strangers would be turned from the door without being fed a complimentary plate of Pasta con Sarde to comfort their spirits and restore them on their daily way. The spiritual connection of cooking and sharing food with friends and loved ones was forever carved in my mind. How was I to make the magic happen?

Twenty-two years of voracious cookbook readings later; the mountains, deserts, valleys, and mini-gardens of northern California; and then, finally and most importantly, Utah, the dream became the reality. My cooking instincts varied from Mediterranean to Southeast Asian. At once a hodge-podge of ethnic varieties, my cooking philosophy evolved to total use of the abundance of fruits and chiles as I settled into the American western environment of Utah, the formerly Hidden West. Fruit-based and chile-based stocks were creative accidents that became creative staples in a somewhat renegade restaurant called JazRanch, which I opened in 1983 in Salt Lake City, Utah.

Fruit-based/fire-spice cooking paved the culinary path to experimenting with bouillons, sauces, vinaigrettes, syrups, creams, coulis, etc., all laden with fruit and frequently subtle but unforgettable fire. Kiwi/tomato, orange/tomato, raspberry/tomato—all served with or without the lacing of a serrano, pasilla, or chipotle—yielded a new direction of sharp and clear flavors for the palate. And why not? Our digestive system most nearly resembles that of animals that are primarily fruit eaters.

Cooking with fruit/fire-spice stocks is for me, finally, a fresh restorative way to feed ourselves as well as each other. Stocks and foods permeated with lightness and sharpness is what the Orient has practiced for centuries—the fruit (sweet) and fire (heat) of life—the yin and yang that we as westerners have tried to leave in the dust. It's time we restore and comfort our souls, sweetly and hotly.

HEADIN' FOR THE SWEET HEAT

Good cookery is the food of a clear conscience.
–Des Essarts

Culinary influences are a little like one's personal taste for fine art—individual and at the same time, hopefully, eclectic. My quirky and ethnocentric food interests have run the gamut from Mediterranean, Native American, Middle Eastern, North African, and Southeast Asian. Stir this all up with living in the hidden west of Utah, where fruit groves and chile bushes thrive in the semiarid conditions, and what evolved was a fruit-based and fire-spice cooking style.

The high desert of Utah, a once-hidden region in the United States, is distinct and separate from the rest of the country. Its primeval mountains, red-rock cliffs, valleys, alpine lakes, and streams impart flavors and fragrances that are raw, wild, tasting truly of the earth.

Mormon ranchers and farmers have known this since settling and working the land in the late nineteenth century. Their pristine lands have produced superb Utah lamb and cheeses, incomparable heavy creams, fruits, vegetables, herbs, freshwater fish, and chiles. By conventional culinary standards emanating from the seat of eating wisdom in Berkeley, California—760 miles west of Utah—and to the throng of newcomers settling here, these flavors may appear bland and unsophisticated on the surface to a jaded palate but are, in truth, sharply pure.

And so, I began to retrain my taste to accommodate these flavors that were not so much new as they were untainted, unprocessed, minimally handled. I wanted to develop cooking techniques that would reveal and enhance these flavors and, hence, create dishes that would be free of the heavy, dominating flavors that were associated with lamb- and chicken-based stocks. In addition, I pursued lighter, more subtle, yet highly flavored methods of barely cooking food to retain its purity. This path brought me to a most welcome creative mistake that was a result of merely maintaining resourcefulness while cheffing and owning JazRanch. In the normal course of tossing vegetable scraps into the stockpot, I began tossing fruit and then chile scraps into that same vessel, which ultimately resulted in fruit, fruit/fire-spice, and/or fire-spice stocks.

Once the fruits were liberated from their previously nonexistent role in making stocks and subordinate role in making sauces, marinades, vinaigrettes, and mustards, unlikely combinations—such as red onion/dates, orange/aniseed, strawberry/ginger, peach/serrano chile, orange/pesto, pear/olive, avocado/kiwi, and on and on—forged new directions of soft and sweet (fruity) with heat (fiery). The magic I had daydreamed about in my childhood was happening. What appeared to be an unchoreographed dance movement became numerous, original, innocent, food compositions with unlimited steps. I was ready. An artist is ready when she or he has the patronage or audience eager to experiment. They were ready too.

Fruited Fiery Broths.....
A Different Cooking Consideration

FRUITED FIERY BROTHS:
A DIFFERENT COOKING CONSIDERATION

Routine in cuisine is a crime.
–Edouard Nignon

HOW FRUIT AND FIRE-SPICE STOCKS EVOLVED

When I first opened JazRanch, I began the daily cooking with the preparation of the usual chicken-based and Utah lamb-based stocks, which simmered away respectively for hours. For some time during the first year of business, I questioned the use of these overprocessed and heavy-tasting stocks that were so pervasively used in the restaurant world as a basis for soups, sauces, and so on. The flavors of these stocks overwhelmed the pure flavors in food. So, the first step was to eliminate lamb stocks. Then on one usually frazzled day in the restaurant kitchen, feeling overworked and silly, I tossed the fruit scraps, destined for compost, into the simmering chicken stock. Oranges, strawberries, peaches, pears, kiwi, raspberries, nectarines—whatever was on the maple prep table made its way into the stockpot. The roasted chicken bones normally simmered in stock for a few hours, but in this instance, I diminished the cooking time to one hour because of the fruit scraps and the notion that I wanted a fresher flavor.

After the stock cooled and was strained, a minimal yet apparent fruit flavor was laced here and there through the chicken stock. So here was a fairly flip cooking accident that became a handier and healthier version of traditional chicken stock.

At that moment, it was joyfully clear that the time had come to rid the stock of what I always felt was the culprit anyway and to permeate the simmering waters with not just fruit scraps but entire fruits.

Once pure fruit stocks were being used, I became instantly aware of the commingling sweet to tart flavors, and by rapidly reducing two or so cups of the stock, a softly intense yet unencumbered sauce emerged. The use of just fruits and their delicate characteristics required the stocks to be simmered fast and furiously in small batches to capture and retain their flavors.

In fact, this method of cooking fruit stocks served two winning purposes: one was a resulting varietal stock of sweet, tart freshness that could be applied to numerous and sundry food possibilities; the other was time—precious time—that was gained for this now-less-frazzled cook. Here was a springboard of creativity. Fruit-based stocks became an integral part of my cooking experience, and what was to ultimately weave its way into this endless palate was none other than the humble and alert chile.

Sweet to tart plus hot equals unrivaled taste and intrigue. In the Asias, where food, flavors, and fragrances assault and flood the senses, the people have known and lived by this for aeons. It was, for this Westerner, a most logical progression to add a minced serrano or New Mexican chile here and there to some of the fruit stocks that would accompany certain special food requests for daring diners. When a serrano chile was added to the stockpot to simmer along with oranges and peaches, what emerged was a fiery yet softly flavored stock that I came to call the fruit/fire-spice mother stock, after the mother stocks used in colorful Thai cooking that provide the base for their hot and fiery dishes.

Fire spice is the variety in life, and food cooked with this in mind motivates and propels the spirit and flesh. The implementation of fruit with fire spice into broths and sauces made such flavors attractive to both willing and unwilling eaters. So the final addition to an orangey broth of a miniscule bit of scotch bonnet chile (having its own fruity, fiery, explosive flavor) or a tiny

Thai chile (with its cleansing, lingering heat) not only provides rounded, balanced flavor but could be anything from Italian to Turkish to Native American to Thai to Creole. The plethora of fruit/fire possibilities was at once invigorating and calming. Time was nigh for tickling tired taste buds, heating the teeth, and, in WoodyAllenesque style, imposing this culinary catharsis upon friends and patrons. Test-driving new dishes always meant opening oneself for darling and undarling criticism. But what better way to learn, live, and benefit from such *au contraire* feedback than by sharing with those initially closed as well as open minds. Fruit/fire steam ahead.

VARIETIES OF FRUIT AND FIRE-SPICE STOCKS

Basic fruit stock can be made with whatever is available from your local farmer, rancher, grocer, and, as a last recourse, your refrigerator. Realistically speaking, the former two are not readily accessible. The latter two are more practical and economical in most instances. We can browse through the produce kiosk at the grocer's and choose anything, depending on where we live, from apple to watermelon. If and when the choices of fruit are sadly minimal, the year-round tireless orange is a most excellent choice for accomplishing the possible and impossible.

If a trip to the grocer's is not a possibility, the refrigerator will have to be the rescue remedy. So whatever fruits that are aging in the bins can be quickly cooked in a saucepan, strained, and tossed through a mound of fettucine that has been sprinkled with lots of fresh herbs and freshly grated Asiago or grana cheese with a bowl of toasted serrano chiles nearby for intermittent fire—food for the angels no matter where they dwell.

True, once fruit is refrigerated it begins the aging process, developing numb and insipid flavor. However, far too much fruit has been tossed in the trash when in fact it could well have been enjoyed in the fettucine dish above. The key and challenge to great, good, delicious cooking is being able to work with whatever ingredients are handy, not excess or ostentation. Improvise with one goal in mind—flavor, and then more flavor.

In the following pages, an attempt has been made to compile a partial list of certain fruits and chiles into their respective seasons and groups with the emphasis on their peak seasons. Obviously, in various areas of America, availability is moot as, oftentimes, any and all fruits and chiles may be in the marketplace. But they do not necessarily have taste due to being in preripening rooms and then being pre-shipped. This, of course, has to do with profit, not quality of human consumption. Let the practice here be caveat emptor.

With this in mind, seasonal is not so rigid, and spring fruits mixed with summer fruits, or fall/winter fruits mixed with out-of-season summer fruits, etc., become possible choices for fruit stock. However, it is best to use fruits and chiles in season because they provide fresh, immediate flavor as well as fair prices.

But please don't be inhibited by the lack of availability of certain fruits/chiles/foods at certain times of the year, especially if a craving for a grilled mushroom/pasilla chile/orange/tomato sandwich kicks in. Move with the mood. Use basic, whole, fresh, stemmed mushrooms and chiles. Mist chiles with fruit stock, thoroughly coating them. No oil please. Grill, broil, or flame-toast them crispy brown. Remove charred skin. Sauté chopped tomato in orange juice until the tomatoes absorb the juice. Press mushrooms/chiles/orange/tomatoes onto fresh Italian bread, or if sliced

14

white bread is all that's in the pantry, use it. You will be forgiven as the mushroom/chile/orange/tomato mixture will briefly elevate the motel pillow to an unworthy position, making it a temporarily edible bread.

In the above example, if the mushroom/chile/orange/tomato sandwich mood struck in summer, then each ingredient is in abundant supply—particularly pasilla chiles and vine-ripened tomatoes. However, assuming the time is winter with no pasillas in sight, a dried ancho chile soaked in fruit stock until soft makes a fine replacement for a toasted sandwich chile. Further, winter tomatoes are usually in chalky and mealy form with basic cardboard flavor. But when the addition of freshly squeezed oranges or packaged orange juice takes place, the plight of the wintry mushroom/chile/orange/tomato sandwich is salvaged. On to fruit and fire-spice times.

TYPES OF FRUIT STOCKS

Basic
Year-Round Fruit
    Green Grape
    Orange
    Strawberry
Multipurpose Fruited Broth
Multipurpose Fruited Sauce
Pureed Fruit

Variations	**Seasonal**
Apple	Seasonal One-Fruit
Berry	Pureed Fruit
Dried Fruit	Fall/Winter Fruit
Ginger	Spring Fruit
Grape	Summer/Fall Fruit
Melon	Mediterranean Fruit
Peach	Tropical Fruit
Pear	Multipurpose Fruited Broth
Watermelon	Multipurpose Fruited Sauce

TYPES OF FIRE-SPICE AND FRUIT/FIRE-SPICE STOCKS

Due to the nature of the chile market, a basic fire-spice mother stock can be used year round with whatever chile is available. During the summer season of chiles, experimentation may ensue with the available varieties by cooking, for example, an Anaheim, pasilla, or piquin stock.

Depending on where one lives in America and the year-round importance of the chile in that particular region, drying fresh chiles on simple waxed paper in the open sun or on a window sill is a way in which these chiles can be used after the plentiful summer harvest. Native Americans in places such as Chinle, Hotevilla, and Tuba City, Arizona still dry their chiles and corn in this way with no concern for bugs. Should this be of some bother to the cook, cover chiles with a finely woven cheesecloth.

Basic	**Seasonal**
Year-round Fire Spice	Seasonal One-Chile Fire Spice
Year-round Fruit/Fire Spice	Seasonal One-Chile Fruit/Fire Spice

FRUIT SEASONS

Fall/Winter
Apple
Banana
Blueberry
Coconut
Cranberry
Date
Dried Fruit
Feijoa
Grapefruit
    Pummelo
    Red
    White
Grape
    Green
    Red
Guava
Kiwi
Kumquat
Lemon
Lime
Mango
Melon
Orange
    Blood
    Fiesta
    Mandarin
    Valencia
Pear
Persimmon
Pineapple
Raspberry
Star Fruit
Strawberry
Tangelo
Tangerine
Tomatillo

Spring
Apple
Apricot
Banana
Blueberry
Date
Dried Fruit
Grape, Green
Grapefruit, White
Kiwi
Lychee
Mango
Nectarine
Oranges
    Blood
    Fiesta
    Valencia
Peach
Pineapple
Strawberry
Tomatillo

Summer/Fall
Apple
Apricot
Banana
Blackberry
Blueberry
Cherry
Currant
    Black
    Red
    White
Date
Dried Fruit
Fig
Gooseberry
Grapefruit, White
Grape
    Black
    Green
    Red
Huckleberry
Kumquat
Lemon
Lime
Lychee
Mango
Melon
Nectarine
Orange
Papaya
Passion Fruit
Peach
Pear
Pineapple
Plum
Prickly Pear
Sapote
    Mamey
    White
Star Fruit
Strawberry
Watermelon
    Red
    Yellow

FRUIT GROUPS

Bramble
Blackberry
Dewberry
Boysenberry
Cloudberry
Currant
   Black
   Red
   White
Dewberry
Elderberry
Gooseberry
Loganberry
Mulberry
Raspberry
Rowanberry
Rhubarb
Rose Hip
Strawberry
Wood Strawberry
Youngberry

Pome
Apple
   Bramley's
   Seedling
   Crispin
   Egremont Russet
   Golden Delicious
   Granny Smith
   Laxton's Superb
   McIntosh
   Orleans Reinette
   Red Delicious
   Rome Beauty
   Worcester Pearmain
Crabapple
Medlar
Pear
   Bartlett
   Comice
   D'Anjou
Quince

Vine
Grape
   Catawba
   Concord
   Emperor
   Muscat
      Black
      Red
      White
   Sweetwater
   Sultana Seedless
   Thompson Seedless
Melon
   Cantaloupe
   Casaba
   Charentais
   Crenshaw
   Honeydew
   Musk
   Ogen
Watermelon
   Sugar Baby
   Tiger

Bush
Blueberry
Cranberry
Huckleberry

Citron
Grapefruit
   Pink
   White
Kumquat
Lemon
Lime
Orange
   Blood
   Mandarin
      Clementine
      Satsuma
   Navel
   Seville
   Valencia
Satsuma
Tangelo
Tangerine
Ugli Fruit

Stone
Apricot
Cherry
   Black
   Royal Anne
   Sour
Nectarine
Peach
Plum
   Burbank
   Cherry
   Damson
   Gaviota
   Greengage
   Santa Rosa
   Victoria

Mediterranean/Tropical
Apple, Custard
Banana
   Dessert
   Plantain
   Red
Coconut
Date
Feijoa
Fig
Ginger
Guava
Jackfruit
Kiwi
Loquat
Lychee
Mango
Olive
Papaya
Passion Fruit
Persimmon
Pomegranate
Prickly Pear
Quince
Star Fruit

Year-Round Chiles

The list below represents basic varieties of chile peppers available year round from California and/or Mexico. In addition, a modest, Scoville Chile Heat Range Scale has been provided to alert the cook to relative hotness.

Fresh
Fresno
Habañero
   Red Savina
   Scotch Bonnet
Jalapeño
New Mexico
Pepperoni
Poblano
Serrano
Yellow

Dried
Anaheim Red
Ancho
de Arbol

Seasonal
Aji
Big Berthas
Black Plum
Cascabel
Chicken Claw
Chinese Multicolor
Chipotle (dried and smoked jalapeño)
Cow Horn
Golden Boy
Korean
Lady Belle
Little Flower
Mexi-Bell
Mirasol
Peter
Red Cherry Hot
Rocoto
Ring of Fire

SCOVILLE CHILE PEPPER HEAT RANGE

Habañero/Red Savina	300,000–400,000	**HOTTEST**
Habañero/Scotch Bonnet	200,000–300,000	
Kumataka	125,000–150,000	
Bird's Eye	100,000–125,000	
Bahamian	100,000–110,000	
Carolina Cayenne	100,000–105,000	
Tabiche	100,000–105,000	
Thai	70,000–80,000	
Chiltecpin	70,000–80,000	
Haimen	70,000–80,000	
Santaka	50,000–60,000	
Red Chile	50,000–60,000	
Tabasco	30,000–50,000	
Chilipiquin	30,000–40,000	
Cayenne	35,000–40,000	
Chile de Arbol	15,000–30,000	
Serrano	7,000–25,000	
Hidalgo	6,000–17,000	
Jalapeño	3,500–4,500	
Ancho Poblano	2,500–3,000	
Anaheim	1,000–1,500	
Coronado	700–1,000	
El Paso	500–700	

FRUITED FIRE IN THE KITCHEN

> . . . since we must eat to live, we might as
> well do it with grace and gusto . . .
> —M. F. K. Fisher

In each of the following recipes for fruit, fruit/fire-spice, and fire-spice stocks, keep a playful attitude when preparing them. Should you have forgotten to add a fruit(s), or added too much fruit or chile, or did not halve the strawberries before cooking, or whatever you deem has been a possible mishap, there are always remedies to undo or outwit the mistake. Simply blend the broth after it has been cooled and strained. Should the Scoville heat level register alarm in the mouth from too much chile . . . have an icy bottle of Qupé Marsanne white wine or beer nearby to sit with, sip, cool down, relax, and then think about converting this out-of-hand fire-spice stock into perhaps ice cubes for red or white gazpacho. No recipe should be taken so seriously that we can't laugh and cry at the same time while cooking away.

I continually envision Babette in the film *Babette's Feast*, wherein she took a 10,000-francs-lottery win and spent every bit of it for the acquisition of fine, fresh ingredients shipped from France to a coastal village in Jutland, Denmark, where she was a cook and servant. This was to be a memorial celebration dinner served to twelve local villagers. A pact was made by the diners not to utter one word about the food, as though they never had the sense of taste. Throughout the exquisitely prepared courses, Babette, in truth a famed Parisian chef, remained in her womb room of a kitchen. Between courses, she would sip fine French wine, champagne, and finally coffee along with fine cognac as she silently inhaled the feeling of feeding their souls. Her simple satisfaction came from her artistic sense to give the villagers her very best efforts in what truly was a holy feast. In the end, they were relaxed, sated, and unknowingly won over by her flavors and single-mindedness to please. Babette's short sermon here emphasizes the gestalt of it all . . . the cooking, serving, and bringing of pleasure to the eater's lips, and that to err in the kitchen, which is often inevitable, is part of the humility and reward contained in the resulting meal. The twist of irony present in Gabriel Axel's food film is that no matter if a person has character or not, if there is a bit of spirit living somewhere in the hidden regions of the heart, lovingly prepared food can but restore and enlarge the human spirit.

In the following pages setting out ingredients and preparation of the fruit and fire-spice stocks, keep Babette's character in mind; that is, keep an open mind when in the kitchen prepping away. Put on some favorite background music for chopping and simmering—sounds such as the diverse soundtrack from the French film *Betty Blue*—and get in the mood for up-tempo fruit and fire-spice cooking.

Fruit/Fire-Spice Stocks

Basic Year–Round Fruit Stock
Two Quarts

REMOVE Stems from 1 lb. seedless **green grapes**, core and quarter 4 medium (1 lb.) ripe comice or d'anjou **pears**, and skin and seeds from 4 **oranges**, placing all in blender-processor.

POUR Fruit puree (5 to 5 1/2 cups) into small stockpot with 5 cups cold water. Simmer/stir on medium-high heat just enough to release fruit flavor into the water, about 15 minutes.

REMOVE From heat, letting fruit stock cool/settle for 10 minutes.

STRAIN Stock into large bowl with fine strainer, gently pressing fruit through, extracting as much fruit liquid as possible. If a more chunky texture is preferred, eliminate this step.

COOL/POUR/ REFRIGERATE Stock in two 1-quart glass jars and use within 2 days. Freeze for long-range use. Separation of the heavier fruit liquid will occur naturally. When ready to use, stir through to redistribute fruit-stock sediment.

COMMENTS Fast and high heat (simmering, not boiling) intensifies stock flavor. Water, however, can be boiled. Perform this cooking step diligently in each stock recipe. Put on Tchaikovsky's "Pas D'Action" from *The Sleeping Beauty* and ease into a few yoga lunge salutes while the simmering fruits do their dance.

This stock, as well as the ones to follow, does best when stored in glass jars. If plastic is to be used, it must be of food-grade high quality as some plastics release chemical residues that make their way into the natural fruit flavor. Minimal microwaving is an option when stock has been frozen. As an alternative, float the container of frozen stock in a bath of hot water until thawed. Freshen flavor when cooking fruit stock with squeezed orange juice, only if needed, adding 1/2 cup per quart of stock.

Bring to simmer rapidly on medium-high heat, about 10 minutes, tasting for even fruit flavor that fills the mouth with sweet tang and tart.

Fruit-stock colors and tastes vary depending on the fruits used as well as what the season brings in flavor. Be a colorist or alchemist by playing with fruit palettes. For example, in the stock above, the color is jade green and brings a beautiful, muted color accent to sauces serving as the background for numerous dishes.

If fruit stock is not strained, the stock will be mottled and slightly pulpy in texture compared to mottled and smooth. This applies to all fruit stocks, and deciding which is preferred by the cook will be a matter of test-driving both approaches. In the instance of banana or tropical fruit stocks, I prefer the cloudy, mottled texture, as it seems to lend itself more to Asian/Southeast Asian sauces, soups, stews, satays, etc. What comes immediately to mind is the Filipino stew *pachero*, containing bananas, wherein a cloudy, mottled broth is desirable.

You will note that I do not use salt or oil in any of the fruit/fire-spice stocks with the exception of the fruited sauces. Only rarely do I find the need to add unsalted, sweet cream butter to the broths, thereby converting them to sauces that hang together a bit more.

Keeping this in mind, adjust flavors to meet your desires for salt, oil or butter. But before doing so, experiment with reducing by cooking the fruit stock down on fast, high heat as instructed above, tasting sporadically for balanced flavors and not extreme fruit-acid tongue attacks. In the instance of converting fruit stocks to sauces as an accompaniment (put the sauce down first, then the food item), think thin (i.e., thin, light frothy sauces, not thick, rich, over-processed resinlike sauces).

USES
Bouillons, broths, sauces; poaching, steaming, basting; and marinades that make for oil-free broiling, grilling, and roasting . . . just ladle and brush uncooked fruit stock onto whatever is being cooked.

Basic Year-Round Orange Stock
Two Quarts

REMOVE
Skins from 8 seedless **oranges** of your choice, quarter and process in blender-processor until reduced to a smooth puree.

PLACE
Orange puree (5 to 5 1/2 cups) in small stockpot with 5 cups cold **water**. Simmer/stir on medium-high heat just enough to release fruit flavor into the water, about 15 minutes.

Fruit/Fire-Spice Stocks

REMOVE   From heat, letting orange stock cool/settle for 10 minutes.

STRAIN   Stock into large bowl with fine strainer, gently pressing orange mass through, extracting as much fruit liquid as possible. If a more chunky texture is preferred, eliminate this step.

COOL/POUR/REFRIGERATE   Stock in two 1-quart glass jars and use within 2 days. Freeze for long-range use. Separation of the heavier fruit liquid will occur naturally. When ready to use, stir through to redistribute fruit-stock sediment.

COMMENTS   Taste test the stock for individual flavor preference. Feel free to add more orange juice (1/2 cup per quart) if the stock does not have a rich orange flavor. This stock should be a pure, straightforward orange essence. It can also be used year round because of the availability of oranges. Depending on the time of year, the tartness/sweetness of the oranges will vary and, hence, the taste test will assure an even orange balance. Should the stock come up too tart, add miniscule bits of superfine sugar and taste until orange sweet/tart flavor is balanced. It is rare that the stock will ever be too sweet, i.e. "too orangey"; but should this occur, squeeze 1/2 lemon or lime to even out flavor. I have often replaced 8 oranges with 16 small satsuma mandarins (the equivalent of 8 oranges) during that rare time when oranges are not acceptable. The color of the mandarin stock was brilliant ochre and the fragrance was wrap-around clementine.

Treat oranges as a staple by having a case handy, if space permits, or a 5 lb. bag around at any given time in either the refrigerator or another cool place.

USES   Bouillons, broths, sauces; poaching, steaming, basting; and marinades that make for oil-free broiling, grilling, and roasting. Spoon fresh or thawed orange stock from glass jar onto fish, fowl, veggies, and cook.

Basic Year-Round Green Grape Stock
One Quart (approximately)

Follow year-round fruit-stock recipe using 2 lbs. **green grapes** and 2 cups **water**.

Basic Year-Round Strawberry Stock
One Quart (approximately)

Follow year-round fruit-stock recipe using 2 lbs. **strawberries** along with their stems and 2 cups **water**. Keep in mind that because of the pulpiness of the strawberry when blended to a puree and then cooked, this stock may require a second straining if a lighter stock is preferred.

Pureéd Fruit Stock
Two Quarts

REMOVE

Stems from 1 lb. seedless **green grapes**, 8 medium **strawberries** (1 cup), core and seeds from 2 **pears**, skin and seeds from 4 **oranges**; then quarter oranges and pears.

PULSE/BLEND

Until smooth puree. Place in small stockpot with 5 cups cold water. Simmer and stir on medium-high heat, just enough to release fruit flavor into the water, about 15 minutes.

REMOVE

From heat and allow stock to cool and settle for 10 minutes.

**COOL/POUR/
REFRIGERATE**

Pureed stock in two 1-quart glass jars and use within 2 days. Freeze for long-range use. Separation of the heavier fruit mass will occur rapidly and naturally because the stock is unstrained. When ready to use, stir through to redistribute fruit sediment.

COMMENT

Because this fruit stock is not strained, it does well for hearty fall/winter dishes but also makes for a most interesting icy cold addition to a summer gazpacho laced with fiery, minced chipotle.

USES

Fall/winter soups, sauces, stews, or stirred through stuffings for moist flavor when baking or roasting.

Seasonal One-Fruit Stock
One Quart

SELECT

Two lbs., one **fruit of your choice**.

ADD

Two-quart recipe for year-round fruit stock, adding 2 cups cold **water** to fruit puree when simmering.

COMMENTS

When using fruits in season, it is wise to taste for true fruit flavors before cooking the stock. Freshly picked ripe fruit is not available year round, and many varieties of fruit often have too much acid or lack flavor, even when ripe, then picked and shipped to the market.

This is the perfect scenario for cooking and adjusting fruit flavors to your taste, keeping in mind there should be a sweet (full fruit) to tart (tinge of sour) balance that may or may not need a pinch of sugar. If fruit flavor is insipid, add freshly squeezed orange juice, starting with 1/2 cup. Two fruits from the same color family can be used here, i.e., **peaches/nectarines**, **strawberries/ raspberries**, **blackberries/boysenberries**, **apricots/ mandarins**, etc.

USES

Bouillons, broths, sauces; poaching, steaming, basting; and marinades that make for oil-free broiling, grilling, and roasting.

Mediterranean- or Tropical-Fruit Stocks
One Quart

Follow seasonal one-fruit-stock recipe or basic year-round fruit-stock recipe replacing with **Mediterranean or tropical fruits** of your choice. Due to the unique and exotic flavors of these stocks, definitely taste as you prep, add, simmer, etc., to achieve a good balance of already unusual flavors. Once again, refer to Chapter 1 for specific fruit seasons or groups.

Multipurpose Fruited Broth
Two Cups

SIMMER

Four cups of **fruit stock** on high heat for 10 minutes. Strain. Serves 2 cups of basic drinking bouillon or broth.

ADD

One cup finely minced and steamed **vegetables** to fruit broth. Serve in 2 large cups or bowls with a toasted baguette slice on broth, some generously grated **Greek cheese** such as mizithra, and then float a honey-dipped **chile** into the broth.

Multipurpose Fruited Sauce
Two Cups

SIMMER

Four cups **fruit stock/orange stock/fire-spice stock** on high heat until reduced by one cup, about 10 minutes.

ADD   Two tablespoons unsalted **sweet butter** and continue simmering on medium-high heat until the sauce barely coats a wooden spoon but is free-flowing, about 10 minutes. Taste test for concentrated flavor.

USES   As a sauce base for fish, fowl, pasta, rice, soups, stews, vegetables, and so on. Enough for 3 or 4 persons.

NOTE   In each of the above recipes, fruited bouillons, broths, sauces, etc., can be converted to fruit and fire spice by carefully adding 1/2 to 1 whole minced **chile** of your choice. In the alternative, prick holes in a fresh whole chile and float in sauce until desired chile flavor is attained; then remove chile.

Basic Year-Round Fire-Spice Stock
One Quart

SEED AND MINCE   One to two **fresh chiles** of your choice, taking care not to touch your eyes during this process.

and/or

CRUMBLE   One to two **dried chiles** of your choice.

BRING   One quart of **water** to a boil. Add 1 minced chile. Simmer for 5 minutes. Taste for chile heat preference.

COOL/POUR/ REFRIGERATE   Fire-spice water and use within 7 days. Lasts indefinitely. Freezing is a waste of time and flavor, as this is such an easy stock to cook up in minutes.

COMMENTS/ USES   This is simply a fire-spice water intended for use as a base for making soups, cooking noodles, soaking and then cooking beans, steaming vegetables, etc., so as to surround the food with chile heat rather than permeate it. Use this stock with caution, and should it come up tasting too hot, add 1/2 cup of **orange juice** or, if handy, 1 cup of any type of **fruit stock**.

Removing seeds from chiles achieves a milder flavor, and chile heat may vary from season to season. Respect, not fear, is the tasting-cooking approach to eating and enjoying the deceptive little critter.

Fruit/Fire-Spice Stocks

Basic Year-Round Fruit/Fire-Spice Stock
One Quart

SIMMER

Four cups **fruit stock** of your choice on medium-high heat for 5 minutes. Remove from heat and strain.

SEED AND
MINCE

One to two fresh **serrano chiles** or chiles of your choice.

and/or

CRUMBLE

One 2" dried **Thai chile**.

ADD

Chiles to fruit stock. Stir. Test taste. Add more chile if desired.

COOL/POUR/
REFRIGERATE

Stock and use within 7 days. Lasts indefinitely. Do not refreeze this stock if fruit stock has been previously frozen.

COMMENT

Fire-spice stocks are dependent on the heat contained in the chiles used. Their staying power and shelf life is longer than fruit stocks. The heat factor will vary from chile to chile, so the gradual addition of fire spice to fruit stocks should be followed closely with test tasting for personal levels of sweat tolerance.

USES

Soups, stews, chilis, bouillons, broths, sauces; soaking beans, poaching, steaming, basting; oil-free broiling, grilling, and roasting.

Seasonal Fruit/Fire-Spice Stock
Two Quarts

This is the simple part. Add 1 to 2 seeded, minced **chile(s)** of your choice per quart to any **fruit stocks** listed in Chapters 1 or 2, and simmer accordingly. Follow remaining recipe steps through COOL/POUR/ REFRIGERATE. If used immediately, freshen flavor with small amounts of **orange juice**. If using frozen and thawed stock, add orange juice when simmering. Depending on the season and chile chosen, taste carefully after adding chile bits to the fruit stock, then add more chile or, alas, none at all.

Each chile has its own special, wild-heat traits. Experiment, prudently keeping in mind that eating chiles is a little like making fresh tortillas. If you don't have 400 years of Mexican or Native American lineage, a natural endurance to chile heat may not be present; but with time, chile tolerance is achieved.

Have *The Whole Chile Pepper Book* handy for information on Scoville units of heat and individual chile pungency. If, however, you're capable of using or eating a habañero, the hottest chile around, then you do not need a chile temperature guide. But if in fact you are charting new chile territory, please refer to the modest Scoville heat guide offering in Chapter 1, page 19. When fresh is not available, dried chiles serve the cook well.

"A Good Cook is the Best Physician" . . . says an old German proverb. "Good" is how it tastes as you savor it; if it truly does have some flavor life in it as it goes down, take the time to notice how it makes you FEEL from the inside out. Good food, good wine, good friends, along with cappuccino and tea, all in Socratic moderation, make for what's left of compassionate spiritual socialization amongst humans. Western civilization has systematically tried to kill this psychic social connection in each of us . . . if you will, an almost eerily orchestrated spiritual famine exists and it is in fact a famine because our spirit hungers for restoration . . ., a reconnection with each other and each other's dormant compassionate spirit.

Cookbooks all too often are merely recipe manuals. Frequently I am approached about sharing my "secret" concerning a particular dish and how, even when I have provided a recipe, it does not taste like what I had served. I balk and laugh at this request and comment because there is no real secret. No matter how accurate an ingredient listing is in a recipe, the main unlisted ingredient is technique-technique-technique. Precise kitchen-testing the recipes ensures eventual tastelessness and does not leave room for spontaneous, soulful flavor. Specifically, recipes get in the way. Your technique is going to be different than mine; therefore, exact ingredients are eyewash if there is no personal style. In cookery as well as in life, individual quality can always be improved.

All recipes in *Headin' for the Sweet* Heat are about humble ingredient offerings intended for your unique technique. To that end, cookbooks are a very pure form of writing that should inspire the inherent playful spirit when cooking seriously or recreationally in one's own kitchen, fireplace, wood-burning stove, or the outdoors. Hopefully the following chapters will serve that end and get the deep juices percolating.

Leeks Limes Lilies
Fruited Vinaigrettes

LEEKS, LIMES, LILIES:
FRUITED VINAIGRETTES

. . . Beulah, peel me a grape . . .
–Mae West

Fruited vinaigrettes have innumerable uses, starting with the most obvious: salads. In early 1979, I developed a "wet seasoning" that truly was no more than a diversified vinaigrette. This product consisted of various fruits, a bit of leek, lime, and extra virgin olive oil spun into an emulsion. It was sold in tenth wine bottles, corked and foil-capsuled in the exact manner as wine is bottled today. Featured as a specialty item exclusively at Marshall Field's in Chicago as well as Macy's and I. Magnin's in San Francisco, it appealed to but a serious few. This wet seasoning-fruited vinaigrette was, for those select few customers, the answer to one-stop shopping in a bottle of Jacquelan. It was used for marinades, salads, sauces, soups. It not only lent flavor when broiling, grilling, sautéing, steaming, roasting, but also tenderized. I admit it . . . I was interested in developing keen flavor that could be used in as many different ways as possible. That small clientele, in retrospect, paved the way to ultimately serving customers on a more one-to-one basis, knowing full well what those needs were to be catered to: flavor with facility.

Years later when JazRanch was opened and I was cheffing for patrons on a one-to-one basis, flavor and facility became paramount in dish after dish. JazRanch diners were also awaiting their form of one-stop shopping after a long hard day doing whatever. That meant dinner, NOW, period.

Fruited vinaigrettes were just another spoke in the fruit/fire-spice moving wheel that helped me to utilize a staple such as the wet seasoning developed way back in 1979. The basic difference in the current recipes is that I use a minimal amount of extra virgin olive oil, and very often, I personally just leave the oil out of the equation because, depending on the fruit, it may mask the honest flavor of the individual fruit about to become the venerable vinaigrette.

When making vinaigrettes, use the fruits of your choice and simply replace fruits for other fruits, using any of my two-cup recipes as your basis. Refer to the fruit and chile groups and seasons in Chapter 1 for general ideas, and then just take off in your own direction. Occasionally reduce the olive oil called for in the recipe to taste exactly what the difference is minus the oil. You betcha, I have used the oil-free vinaigrette as a fragrant, cleansing bath addition with chunks of ginger floating here and there to soothe my day's end. Have no restrictions with fruit uses as they have soothing, restorative qualities that affect the physical inner and outer self.

In all recipes, use fresh herbs, any herbs, profusely. Strip them from their stems (2 Tbs.), and whisk or pulse-blend them into the fruited vinaigrette. When either the vinaigrettes or mustards come up tasting too tart/sharp, adding more olive oil will round the flavors out. These little Easter Egg-colored wonders hold up reasonably well under cool room temperatures as well as actual refrigeration, not to speak of their spartan dollar-and-cents sense.

Lastly, and most importantly, these recipes have been kitchen-tested, but not in the ideally perfect "let's publish a cookbook" restaurant manner. That method of kitchen-testing is not the real world. Each of the following recipes have been prepared in an impeccable home-kitchen setting with an actual hardworking, busy human having just enough time to cook up some soul food for the body and spirit—no sous chefs, salad chefs, or pastry chefs slaved away at perfection with state-of-the-culinary-art equipment for this kitchen party—just me and a few sous guardian angels. Freshness, simplicity, and relative ease have been formatted into the recipes so as to provide the cook with a vinaigrette springboard from which to leap. So, make an inspiring arrangement of leeks and lilies in a pitcher of water and have the limes ready to roll and squeeze.

Fruited Vinaigrettes

Apple or Dried Apple
One Cup

PEEL/CORE One Granny Smith or large **apple** of your choice or 3/4 cup dried unsulphured apples. Use peels for fruit stock.

BLEND One cup pure, unsweetened, and, if possible, unfiltered **apple juice**, juice of 1/2 **lime** and 2 Tbs. extra **virgin olive oil** with the apple until smooth.

POUR Into glass bottle and refrigerate. It will be a celadon green color. When ready to use, shake and let stand at room temperature.

SIMPLY Toss and coat shredded **carrots** or any **greens** or steamed **vegetable** of your choice. Spread on a large, inviting **tortilla** and—that's right—top it with a toasted dangerous **chile** of your choice; now roll it up, it doesn't have to be neat to eat. Hey—you forgot the freshly pressed **raspberries** to spike the Tecate.

COMMENT The dried apple version is pulpier and yields less than the fresh apple. In fact, this makes for a far more interesting applesauce than vinaigrette. If desired, extend dried apple vinaigrette with 1/4-cup increments of apple juice until preferred consistency is reached.

Apricot or Dried Apricot
Two Cups

HALVE/PIT/ BLEND Four **apricots** and/or 3/4 cup dried unsulphured apricots with one cup **orange juice** and 2 Tbs. extra **virgin olive oil** until smooth.

POUR Into glass bottle and refrigerate. When ready to use, shake and let stand at room temperature a bit.

SIMPLY Make some mashed **potatoes** whatever way you deem the easiest, pile them on a plate, make a deep well in the center, and generously pour in the apricot vinaigrette.

Float some of my infamous singed **garlic chips** in the well **(see p. ??)**. Use a jumbo straw for uncontrollable gratification. Where's the turkey hash?

COMMENT Taste test for pure apricot flavor. I have omitted the lime here, but add it back in if it's needed to furnish just a bit of tart. The color of this vinaigrette, depending on the apricots, can look like the sunlit ochre buildings all through Italy.

Cherry Radish
Two Cups

PIT/BLEND   One-half cup **cherries** of your choice, 6 large **red radishes**, 1 cup **orange juice**, 1 **lime**, 2 Tbs. extra **virgin olive oil** until smooth.

POUR   Into glass bottle and refrigerate. When ready to use, shake and let stand at room temperature.

SIMPLY   Float your basic baby **zwieback toasts** on a hearty **onion** or **black bean soup** with a dollop of **yoghurt**, **sunflower seeds**, and then a spoonful of cherry radish vinaigrette . . . or toss through a **spinach salad** along with 1 finely ground piece of zwieback toast. Get loose and messy—eat with your fingers.

COMMENTS   Depending on variety, cherries should be dark, juicy, and ripe or golden, juicy, and ripe, but fully sweet. This vinaigrette works as a summer/fall marinade for broiling, grilling, roasting.

Mango Chile
Two Cups

PEEL/PIT   One **mango**, 1 cup **orange juice**, 1 **lime**, 2 Tbs. extra **virgin olive oil** until smooth.

POUR   Into glass bottle and refrigerate. When ready to use, shake and let stand at room temperature a bit.

FLAME-TOAST   A **red chile** of your choice. Blend with 1 oz. **raisins**, 1 Tbs. **peanuts**, and 1 tsp. **sugar** to a paste. Stir this through mango vinaigrette. Broil skin-on **chicken breasts**. When done, remove skins, cut meat in small pieces, and add 2 Tbs. or so of mango-chile mixture. Have warm **corn tortillas** or soft **lavash** smeared with roasted **garlic paste** . . . a good way for new eaters of chile to break into fruit and fire-spice taste sensations. Eyes watering yet?

COMMENT   A tropical- , Asian- , perhaps Indonesian-tasting kind of vinaigrette—especially once the chile paste is added. Use the chile paste separately and sparingly from the mango vinaigrette so as to enjoy the unique flavors of both. Try this with papaya, yellow or green.

Fruited Vinaigrettes

Melon Chile
One-and-a-half Cups

SKIN/SEED One-half small **cantaloupe**, **honeydew**, or **charentais melon**.

BLEND One **lime**, 1/4 small **red onion**, 2 Tbs. extra **virgin olive oil** until smooth.

POUR/STRAIN Into glass bottle and refrigerate. The mixture will be cantaloupe-colored. When ready to use, shake and let stand at room temperature.

OR SIMPLY Pour into two bowls. Add a palmful of **thyme** pulled from its stem. Wrap a few **grissinis** with **prosciutto** or **pancetta**. Shave a few thin pieces of **grana** or **Asiago cheese** onto melon soup. Swirl grissini in soup and savor the crunch of the bread stick and the cured prosciutto taste against cold, pure bursts of melon. The prosciutto-grissini addiction . . . can never get enough.

COMMENT Melons in season make for very delicate and refreshing fruit vinaigrettes in summer/fall. They do well with greens such as butter and romaine lettuces, frisee, radicchio, and a peppery rocket.

Orange Sun-Dried Tomato
Two Cups

SOAK Six sun-dried **tomato** halves in 1 cup **orange juice** at room temperature until soft.

BLEND Softened, oranged, sun-dried tomatoes with 2 Tbs. extra **virgin olive oil** until it becomes a smooth emulsion.

POUR Into glass bottle and refrigerate. When ready to use, shake and let stand at room temperature.

BRUSH On day-old Italian or sourdough **bread**, and broil. If some **scallions** are handy, chew on a few along with this tomato toast and drink a glass of San Giovese vino.

COMMENT This vinaigrette should be an intense tomato flavor rounded out by the orange juice. If not tart enough, a dash of **balsamic vinegar** will tarten and sweeten. If too tart, add **virgin olive oil** until the edge is gone.

Peach
Two Cups

**PEEL/PIT/
BLEND**

One ripe **peach** or **nectarine** (or play and use both), 1 cup **orange juice**, 1 Tbs. **rosemary**, 2 Tbs. extra **virgin olive oil** until smooth. Use skins for fruit stock.

POUR

Into glass bottle and refrigerate. It will be a true pale peach color. When ready to use, shake and let stand at room temperature.

COOK

One cup **couscous** or **pastina** and strain. Quick-fry a handful of **cherry tomatoes** coated in this vinaigrette until soft. Fork-mash tomatoes in bowl. Stir a couple tablespoons of the peach vinaigrette and cherry tomatoes through couscous or pastina. Grate a storm of **fontinella** on top (yes, this is a softer cheese to use, but it vaporizes instantly into the couscous/pastina). Baby yourself with this baby food.

COMMENT

Fresh peaches can be replaced with dried peaches (l/2 cup) and/or fresh nectarines. If need be, round out flavor with olive oil and **sugar** as is the case in each vinaigrette recipe. This vinaigrette can be spooned onto **focaccia bread**, topped with slivered **onions**, and broiled until onions singe, thereby releasing a sweet flavor. Dip hot focaccia into vinaigrette and coo with pleasure.

Pear Ginger
Two Cups

**PEEL/CORE/
BLEND**

One fresh **pear** of your choice or 3/4 cup dried pears, one 1"-long piece of peeled fresh **ginger**, 1 medium **garlic bud**, 1 cup **orange juice**, 2 Tbs. extra **virgin olive oil** until smooth.

POUR

Into glass bottle and refrigerate. When ready to use, shake and let stand at room temperature for a bit.

SIMPLY

Pick up a couple of **smoked trout** at your local deli to use with this vinaigrette. It is a favorite of this cook. Ladle l/4 cup of pear-ginger mix onto small plate—use base of ladle to spread evenly—and place trout on vinaigrette.

Make some marshmallow-sized **croutons**—BIG—and surround trout. Charred petite **chiles** complete another finger-food meal.

Fruited Vinaigrettes

COMMENT   Note that I did not include straining this vinaigrette. The fine bits of pear contribute far too much flavor. It complements curries as not only a wet condiment but also after aromatizing East Indian spices, commingling the pear-ginger mix with the intensely heated and crushed spices.

Because this vinaigrette is so-o-o tasty, I double the recipe to have lots handy during pear season as well as doing a mini-bottling to have the summer pear-ginger vinaigrette available in late fall/winter. The juice of 1 **lime** in the BLEND step is optional depending on pear sweetness.

Strawberry
One to Two Cups

BLEND   One brimming cup **strawberries** with stems (about 4 medium strawberries), 1 cup **orange juice**, 1 large **garlic bud**, 2 Tbs. extra **virgin olive oil** until smooth.

POUR   Into glass bottle and refrigerate. When ready to use, shake and let stand at room temperature for a bit.

SIMPLY   Toss in handfuls of **thyme** or **basil** or **chervil** or **marjoram** or 1 tsp. dried spices such as freshly ground **aniseed**, **cumin**, **fennel**, or roasted **sesame** for exotic-tasting **greens**. Cut greens into chiffonade (1/2" ribbon strips) and coat gently. Pile onto a platter with a dense, dark country **bread**, a chunk of **Gorgonzola Dolce cheese**, and a crisp **Anaheim chile**—gets the salsa dance spirit movin'.

COMMENT   The tireless, most versatile fruit vinaigrette, de rigeur strawberry vinaigrette never, ever gets boring. It is the better berry, and because of its year-round availability, it is more inviting in stocks, vinaigrettes, and mustards than most fruits. It is considered a freak fruit by botanists, as is the pineapple, because it grows to be an enlarged fleshy receptacle covered with numerous, very small, embedded "achenes" (or seeds). During its peak season of April, May, and June, strawberry flavor is at its most fragrant. No matter, it never loses its charm.

NOTE   When necessary, adjust its real berry flavor with **lime**, **olive oil**, or **sugar**.

No Stranger to Sweat
Fruit fire Mustards

CHAPTER 4

NO STRANGER TO SWEAT:
FRUIT-FIRE MUSTARDS

. . . what doubts the Son of God to sit and eat?
these are not fruits forbidden . . .
–John Milton
Paradise Regained

My loving grandfather Santo could always be counted on for treasures carried in his pants' pockets, or two-inch hardened cylinders of pure honey wrapped in waxed paper and hidden somewhere in the house for one of the three of us to find. I was the oldest and always experienced the thrill of finding that hiding place. Santo was the epitome of androgynous charm and possessed gifted tastebuds. He continually served us delicious yet basic tastes at most meals with no fuss but great style . . . something he shared in common with my equally loving grandmother Francesca. Their freshly made ricotta, slapped and smeared on thick fresh Italian bread with pressed berries and fine muscovado sugar sprinkled on top, was holy communion.

But the confection I remember best was his *mustarda di frutta* (fruit mustard)—that Italian flavor anomaly that I reflect back on and know that this was what started me on the path of strangely sweet but sharp. A fruit mustard could include any number of fruits—such as apricots, dates, fresh or dried figs, peaches or pears—mashed and preserved in a lemon, lime, or orange syrupy liquid with crushed mustard seeds here and there. This, he frequently reminded me, was an Italian confection dating back to the 1500s that was and still is eaten today in the same manner, spread on bread. Every now and then, an unlikely chile would be minced into his mustard, and Santo's lessons on sweat began. These next few modest recipes are the evolution of those lessons.

Italian Fruit Mustard—*Mostarda di frutta*
One to Two Cups

**PEEL/CORE/
PIT**

Four fresh or 3 dried **figs**, 1 **peach**, 1 **pear**, and pulse-blend with juice of 1/2 **lime**, 2 Tbs. unflavored **Dijon mustard**, 2 Tbs. **orange juice** until smooth. Add more orange juice if emulsion is too thick.

PLACE

In glass or ceramic jar for morning, noon, and night easy-eating access.

USE

As a jam, relish, chutney (by mincing a small **chile** into fruit mustard), condiment, flavor enhancer, or accompaniment to whatever flight of fancy presents itself. Or just spread the fruit mustard on the top of a plain pizza crust and bake crispy. Fill a raw Anaheim or chile of your choice with the fruit mustard, and eat along with your fruit mustard pizza. Don't bother to cut the pizza, just pull it apart and enjoy as they did in the 1500s—an image that sets in motion thoughts of Patrick Suskind's novel *Perfume*—caveman style tastes better.

COMMENT

Use any fruits, fresh or dried, of your choice, just mixing and matching. Play with adding fresh **lemon juice** instead of orange. When possible, use **mustard seeds** and/or an unflavored, unsalted, high-quality, stone-ground mustard, adding gradually and taste testing accordingly. If **balsamic vinegar** is used, the mustard color produced is dark and rich . . . best to use for an all dried-fruit mustard. Eliminate orange juice, and taste to determine if juice of **lime** is needed. This fruit mustard is an acquired taste, don't be too quick to pass judgment on its unique flavor.

Fruit-Fire Mustards

Apple
One Cup

PEEL/CORE   One large or 2 small tart **apples** and blend with 8 Tbs. **orange juice**, 2 Tbs. unflavored **Dijon mustard** until relatively smooth.

PLACE   In glass or ceramic jar.

USE   On greens of all kinds, as well as tomato/onion or potato salads, or tossed through a seafood salad, or used to marinate seviche. This very appley-green flavor is so fresh and cleansing, it could even be mixed with sparkling water and a cucumber-spear stirrer as a swift pick-me-up as long as there is a brimming bowl of freshly baked sweet potato chips nearby.

COMMENT   This mustard need not be confined to tart apples. Should the apples be sweet, add the juice of 1/2 **lime** before adding **orange juice** for flavor consistency. This mustard will not be as thick as most mustards—apples and citrus fruits have more water content—but in fact, the lighter texture of this is not at all objectionable because of the many little bits of apple floating throughout.

Banana
Three-fourths Cup

PEEL/BLEND   One medium **banana**, juice of 1/2 **lime**, 2 Tbs. unflavored **Dijon mustard** until smooth and sticky tasting.

PLACE   In glass or ceramic jar.

USE   In tropical or Southeast Asian dishes. Swirl a tablespoon or so through soups and stews at the last minute after removing from heat. This is a unique mustard sauce for raw and steamed vegetables or a very warm and chewy soft pretzel. Pass the Vernor's ginger ale.

COMMENT   So easy, try it blindfolded.

Cranberry (dried)
Three-fourths Cup

MOISTEN

One-half cup **dried cranberries** and 1/4 cup **raisins** or **dried cherries** for 10 minutes in 6 Tbs. **orange juice**. Blend with juice of 1/2 **lime** and 3 Tbs. unflavored **Dijon mustard** until smooth.

PLACE

In glass or ceramic jar.

USE

On Thanksgiving mashed potatoes, turkey, ham, all those autumn/winter-kinda-feeling foods. Prick a hole in a flaky popover and drop a teaspoon of this mustard into its eggy cavern for good, old-fashioned, down-home flavor. A cranberry mint spritzer is definitely in order.

COMMENT

Dried fruit mustards are perfect condiments to get the palate accustomed to a slow, easy heat on the tongue while the fruit keeps the sweat from actually happening —tongue teasers for more perspiring times.

Date
One-fourth to One-half Cup

BLEND

Ten small **dates**, juice of 1/2 **lime**, 2 Tbs. unflavored **Dijon mustard**, 2 Tbs. **orange juice** until smoothly viscous.

PLACE

In glass or ceramic jar.

USE

In Mediterranean and Middle Eastern dishes . . . a pure delicious date mustard tasting like a semi-exotic, Bavarian-style, sweet/tart mustard. Pile some really fresh dates such as bahris into a small bowl; spread some brie on onion matzos, topping with date mustard. Bite that date and then that matzo. Finish with Turkish coffee, and turn that cup over onto its saucer when done—the coffee grounds need to tell their story.

COMMENT

Such a provocative, sensual, fudgey-like fruit. Memories of eating Tunisian stem dates in Vicari, Sicily, with thin-skinned, sweet and juicy tarocco oranges from Palagonia, Sicily. I can't say enough good about dates.

Fruit-Fire Mustards

Fig (dried)
One-fourth to One-half Cup

BLEND   Four de-stemmed dried **figs**, juice of 1/2 **lime**, 4 Tbs. **orange juice**, 2 Tbs. unflavored **Dijon mustard** until smooth.

PLACE   In glass or ceramic jar.

SIMPLY   Toast a couple of slices of thick honey-wheatberry bread. Spread mustard on toast with some good quality Italian ham or baked American ham, lettuce, tomato, and crispy, grilled onions. Rev up the Harley—this is road food.

COMMENT   Ranks up there with date mustard. Must be the Mediterranean mythology surrounding their centuries of delicate propagation.

Kiwi
One Cup

PEEL   Two **kiwi** and blend with 4 small **dates**, 2 Tbs. unflavored **Dijon mustard**, one 1"-long, **fresh serrano chile** until smooth.

PLACE   In glass or ceramic jar.

COAT   A bowl of cut-up grilled **chicken sausages**. Load the fork with one or two at a time, feeding each other and breaking some French bread every now and then— well, maybe a bit more often than every now and then—to settle those chile tongues down.

COMMENT   This is not objectionable serrano heat; in fact, chew on an additional one while eating away. Why is it an apple a day instead of a chile a day? Chiles work harder at keeping bodily resistance where it should be, in check and ready for battle.

Orange
One to One-and-a-half Cups

**PEEL/
QUARTER** Two medium seedless **oranges** and blend with a 1/2"-by-2" strip of **orange zest**, 2 Tbs. unflavored **Dijon mustard**, one 1"-long **serrano chile**. Again, this citrus mustard will not be thick in consistency. Try making with 1 orange and same remaining ingredients for moderately intense fruit and fire.

PLACE In glass or ceramic jar.

USE With delicate vegetables and angel hair pasta, pastina, orzo, acini di pepe. Because this is a light mustard, it does well with a main-course mounding platter of Chinese pea sprouts overlaced with sesame oil, or steamed and broiled celeriac strings with freshly ground celery seed scattered on top, or thinly sliced carpaccio with peppery rocket greens sitting in the center of the plate, waiting to be fingered and rolled inside the carpaccio concoction. Eat this with a shot of Napa Valley grappa.

COMMENT This is a thinner mustard and can double for a vinaigrette. Experiment with the same amounts, only with tangerines, mandarins, clementines, etc.

Papaya (green)
One Cup

PEEL/SEED One large ripe green **papaya** and blend with 2 Tbs. unflavored **Dijon mustard**, and an optional 1" **serrano chile** until smooth.

PLACE In glass or ceramic jar.

TOSS Steamed shrimp, peanuts, broken chunks of uncooked ramen noodles, and garlic chips together with this sweet/hot, tongue-tolerant mustard. Eat it immediately or forget about it until the next day, ´cause it will taste just as good, and those crazy ramen noodles will be just the right chewy texture. Maybe throw in some split green grapes too and a side of Chinese donuts, a kind of Chinese rice-flour bread.

Fruit-Fire Mustards

Plum
One Cup

PEEL/PIT Two **plums** and blend with 2 Tbs. unflavored **Dijon mustard**, one 1" **serrano chile** until smooth.

PLACE In glass or ceramic jar.

COMMENT In addition to the plums used above in the mustard emulsion, add bits of fresh plums when in season to further accentuate subtle plum flavor. This is an all-purpose mustard, particularly in Oriental dishes.

Raspberry
One Cup

BLEND One cup **raspberries** (or berries of your choice), juice of 1/2 **lime**, 1–1/2"-by-2" strip of **orange zest**, 2 Tbs. unflavored **Dijon mustard** until smooth. Taste for even, sweet berry flavor. If too tart, pinch and blend a bit of **sugar**.

PLACE In glass or ceramic jar.

BRUSH Generously on outside of 1 lb. of tender pork, and sear; then roast at 400 degrees for 40 minutes until juices run clear when meat is pierced. Slice into medallions and place in a circle on outer edge of plate. Pile some big thymed croutons in center. This is when it would be perfect if a 1986 Ridge York Creek zinfandel miraculously appeared as a companion to enjoy this fireside meal. Ah well, grab any red.

COMMENT Do experiment with the many berry-mustard possibilities that are deep, rich colors.

High Peasant
Eats . . .
Appetizers

CHAPTER 5

HIGH-PEASANT EATS:
APPETIZERS

> . . . people ought to start tasting with their mouths
> and not their heads . . .
> –David Riley, M.D./Homeopath

With the emergence of California cuisine in 1976, largely due to Alice Waters' unrelenting culinary calling, it would have appeared that perhaps America could well have been on a better eating track. Alas, in 1996 eating for so many is still the cardboard cuisine experience. In some unfortunate twist of culinary fate, eating and dining well seems to be available to a privileged few.

And considering what was being served upstairs in the cafe at Chez Panisse—not just delicious, solid peasant food but encouraging solidarity amongst friends and comrades—The Berkeley California Cuisine Experiment was picked up by others and absorbed into the mainstream to become the profitable food hustle story of the last two decades. What started out as peasant food was no longer affordable and, hence, unavailable for those for whom it was intended—the hardworking classes in America. And weren't the hippies supposed to be the answer to revolutionary peasants? Wait a minute—hippie to yuppie, Che Guevara to Chez Panisse—just exactly what happened here? A *cucina povera*, the "cuisine of the poor," became a *cucina ricca*, the "cuisine of the rich."

Okay, it's time to rethink all this and *mangiare*. Eat—like Balzac and the rest of the peasants—with modest money and much gusto in the act of cooking. Get resourceful with freshness.

Release the sentimental chemicals. Be a child and pass it on to the children. Don't buy into the social garlic of our times—no odor, no taste, inedibly edible, and affordable—such a cruel snake-oil salesman trick. It's time to reflect on the broken peasant food cart and regain our dignity.

Eat, eat, don't stop eating. Or, as spoken in Italy, *mangia! mangia!* These are expressions of affection and just another way of saying, ". . . it tastes good, yes? then, eat, enjoy, and feel good . . ."

Nothing brings greater joy to this cook than to see the changing face of a satisfied and restored eater during and after a meal, particularly a peasant meal. Peasant food is still closest to the soul—comfort food—whether it's a bowl of Neapolitan priest stranglers *(gnocchi)* or a handful of Greek suicide cookies *(kourambiedes)*. It has texture, form, flavor, and in true peasant tradition, gives a bit of fight in the mouth, al dente, to the tooth. No introspective psychology or hidden meanings here. Exit the therapy offices immediately. Head for the closest grub and ethics cafe. Sit and share life with a friend who cares rather than someone who is charging $100 an hour to sit and stare. Head for the high-peasant eats. Pass that pasta puttanesca, pizza furioso, or those anchovy olives. Long live the contadini. Retool your peasant wagon.

Fig Tapenade
Serves Four to Six

PIT

One cup **gaeta** or **Italian black olives**, or 1/2 cup Greek kalamata **olive paste**, 1 Tbs. extra **virgin olive oil**, 1 rinsed **anchovy fillet**, 1 medium **garlic clove**, 5 de-stemmed **dried calmyrna figs**, juice of 1 **lime**, 2 tsp. of pure **fruit syrup** or **fruit preserves** of your choice. Blend these ingredients until smooth. Makes 1 cup.

PLACE

In glass or ceramic jar and allow to settle for several hours. Then retaste to even flavors, if needed.

SERVE

On any dense country bread that has been grilled, broiled, or cooked in the fireplace. Spread on a thin baked pizza, adding bits of dried chiles. Once made and kept handy for food emergencies, this can be served with bread sticks or very thinly sliced croutons to unexpected and unsuspecting guests unless, of course, it gets eaten long before such an arrival.

Poet's Anchovy Toast
Serves Four

SLICE

Diagonally four 1/2"-thick pieces of **Italian bread** or thinly slice 1/2 of a skinny **baguette** for smaller, more manageable mouthfuls.

MASH

One small tin of flat **anchovy fillets** from Morocco (King Oscar brand will do; however, the anchovies in glass have truer anchovy flavor) with a pinch of **cloves** until smooth. Stir in 2 Tbs. **créme fraîche** or high-quality **sour cream**. Makes 1/2 cup. Mound on bread and broil until edges are slightly burnt. As The Wondrous Elizabeth David once said, ". . . hardly enough anchovy to provoke a mild thirst, let alone a lust." A very cold German domtal will at least temper the thirst for those who are fainthearted anchovy eaters.

COMMENT

From afar, I envision Cavafy—a great love poet of the twentieth century—-sitting in a Greek seaside cafe, eating poet's toast made with anchovies caught straight from the sea and broiled whole with just bits of garlic, parsley, and lemon.

Salsa Jacquelina

Serves Four

PEEL/CORE   And finely mince 1 medium **pear**, 1 **serrano chile** or 1 small fresh **red jalapeño**, 1 small **red onion**, 1 medium **garlic clove**, one 2"-piece **orange zest**.

CUT   Finely 2 **roma tomatoes**.

MIX   Juice of 1 **lime**, 1 **orange**, 1/2 tsp. **superfine sugar**, 2 tsp. rinsed **capers** or **green peppercorns**, stirring until blended.

SPOON   All ingredients into one bowl, mixing well. Makes about 2 cups.

PLACE   In glass jar. When ready to use, serve with plenty of **fresh mint** or crushed **cumin seed**.

COMMENT   Fruit Salsa alla Italiana-Mexicana . . . to eat with a pequito bean mash, Anasazi beans, cranberry beans, canellini beans, black beans, or just your special bean dip. And for the little extra zing, add the serrano and the jalapeño to the salsa to, in fact, dance the salsa.

Singed Garlic Chips
Serves Two to Four

REMOVE   Chaff from one medium whole **garlic bulb** and slice in thin chips from vertical tip to base of clove.

DRY BROIL OR SAUTÉ   In 1/4 cup extra **virgin olive oil** on medium heat, tossing and turning chips until golden brown with singed edges.

REMOVE   With slotted spoon and place on absorbent towel to pat dry residual oil.

PLACE   In sealed container.

TURN   On the radio and listen to some dinner jazz. Mound the singed garlic chips on some fresh Italian bread. Drizzle a bit of extra virgin olive oil on the chips. Pour a glass of pignoletto for friends and family. Forget dinner. Makes enough for 2 to 4, depending on the amount of Mediterranean in their background.

USE   For quick nibbling or add to any and all dishes of your choice. Me, I have gone as far as dipping the chips in milk chocolate—it's the ancient Italian in me.

COMMENT   Have a constant stash of these little treasures available for producing wide-eyed grins and incessant questions. Do not be afraid to burn edges as this releases a sweet hit of flavor in the chips, kind of similar to caramelizing.

Singed Ginger Chips
Serves Two to Four

FOLLOW   Directions above using one 5"-long, peeled **ginger root** sliced into thin chips. **Sesame oil** can replace olive oil if handy. Commentary above also applies to ginger chips except that, depending on how much Oriental is in one's background, more ginger may be needed. Drizzle a **fruit syrup** or **fruit honey** over the singed ginger chips and store in glass. This is an original sweet-heat confection to be eaten out of the palm of your hand as a momentary appetizer.

Singed Onions
Serves Four

SLICE   Two large **red onions** into thin crescents. Bring extra **virgin olive oil** to medium heat, add onions, and begin **sautéing**. Keep separating and redistributing onions to crisp and singe evenly. This is a seemingly slow process as this cooking is about burnishing, and then, suddenly, the onions are singed on their edges.

REMOVE   With slotted spoon and place on towels to absorb any excess oil. Fork-fluff gently.

PLACE   In glass jar and store in a cool, dry area for use at any time.

SERVE   Handfuls on pasta with grated cheese, on French bread as in the singed-garlic tradition, on a baked pizza; floating on soup, sprinkled through salads, stuffed in tomatoes or sweet peppers, or on cardboard . . . because that's how good they taste. How about steaming a corn tortilla and filling it with the singed onions, rolling it tightly, as in flauta-tightly, and have a good fruit salsa ready for dippin' such as Salsa Jacquelina (see p. 48). I don't want any beer with this onion flauta—I want an icy late harvest '85 Hacienda riesling. Sounds like a Tesuque, New Mexico, impromptu kinda snack.

Smoked Trout Club Sandwich with Apple Horseradish
Serves Two or Three

REMOVE

Bones and head from a 10-to-12-oz. smoked or cooked **trout**. Save these fish parts for a fish/fruit/chile court bouillon. Gently lift trout flesh from skin and place in mixing bowl.

ADD

Just enough **virgin olive oil** and **fresh lime juice** to lightly coat trout. Set aside.

PEEL/CORE

One medium tart or sweet **apple** of your choice and mince finely. Place minced apple in another bowl, squeeze juice of 1/2 **lemon** over fruit, and toss. Let sit for 10 minutes.

PEEL/MINCE

Very finely one 1–1/2"-long piece **horseradish root**. Mix with **apple/lemon** thoroughly. Taste to round out flavors—**olive oil** to take off edge, **sugar** to balance sweet/tart/hot.

SLICE

French **baguette** on an angle in 1/2" thickness for six pieces of bread, and toast darkly. Mound trout, then apple horseradish equally on 3 toast halves, topping with other halves of toast. If preferred, eat apple horseradish as a condiment rather than as part of the Trout Club. Red and yellow **cherry tomatoes** are needed here for additional bursts of flavor in the mouth.

COMMENT

This is my version of a Trout Club, but I use a sliced bread such as Pacific Bay Sweet Ranch (Utah) or Pepperidge Farm very thinly sliced white (the East). White can be used to stack the sandwich just like a bacon, lettuce, and tomato; i.e., toast, trout, toast, trout, toast, and cut into the club wedge. Serve with cloudy, unfiltered, in-season, Sebastopol apple juice—pitchers of it.

Walnut Olive Rusks
Serves Six to Ten

BEAT/BLEND

Four large **eggs**, 1/2 cup **superfine sugar**, 1 Tbs. finely minced **orange zest** until creamy. Gently blend 2 cups **flour** into egg mixture. Stir in 1/2 cup coarsely chopped **walnuts**, 1/2 cup crushed black Italian **olives** or 1/2 cup Greek kalamata **olive paste** or, if handy in the cupboard, 1/2 cup of fig tapenade. Mix well, and then hand form the dough, scraping up all bits and pieces into dough until it's a smooth ball. **Butter** and flour two 10"-by-3 1/2" loaf pans.

DIVIDE And shape into two loaves. Press gently into loaf pans, and bake in preheated 300-degree oven for 45 minutes. Check to see if dough consistency is ready to cut. If not, bake for another 5 to 7 minutes, checking texture of dough. Remove from oven and carefully cut into 3/4"-thick slices in pan with sharp serrated knife, wiping knife clean every five slices; yields twenty-four 3/4" slices. Return to oven, dropping temperature to 250 degrees Fahrenheit and cook for 2 hours. Remove pan from oven and carefully lift each slice out with a butter knife. Place all slices on a cookie sheet and return to oven for 1 last hour until hard and crisp.

USE For any sailor's soup, stew, antipasto, maybe a Sunday night singed-onion soup—with mandarin and a hit of Pernod—or just sporadic, daytime or nighttime, adult zwieback feedings.

White Vegetable Broilcakes
Serves Four to Six

STEAM One coarsely cut, medium **cauliflower** head and 4 medium **parsnips** until soft. Puree with 1 cup **buttermilk** or 1/2 cup of **fruit stock**.

ADD Six finely ground **matzo crackers**, 1 tsp. minced **orange zest**, one 1/2"-by-1/2" piece of fresh **ginger** and blend until smooth and malleable for forming patties. Season with dashes of **sea salt** and **cracked pepper**.

FORM Into irregular flat patty shapes. Brush lightly with extra **virgin olive oil** and broil until crusty on each side. Simmer 2 cups of **fruit stock** on high heat for 10 minutes. Ladle the stock onto the plates; set 2 broilcakes free onto the fruit stock. A mixed tumbler of picholine olives and raspberries, quick.

COMMENT I have layered sausage and fennel patties atop these simple broilcakes, and spread the surface with a dried-fruit mustard. It's stick-to-the-ribs autumn food that gets washed down with plenty of sparkling water spiked with orange.

Garden in a Pot...
Soups and Stews

GARDEN IN A POT:
SOUPS AND STEWS

> . . . we all ought to remind ourselves that food is or was
> a living thing . . .
> –Colman Andrews

Grazing in a summer garden always brings to mind and mouth how much better food tastes when it is eaten fresh from the soil. Nature in its pristine pot, the earth. Virginal food—untouched, unprocessed, filled with clear, free, spiritual energy—the way the food chain was intended to live in natural harmony. There is but a fortunate few who enjoy the pure and healthy benefits of eating in this idealistic way. That is not to say that one cannot come as close to freshness and untainted or minimally processed foods as possible. It takes a little time, and to do so is to be keenly aware and respectful of the origins of the food we so often take for granted.

In Caroline Walker Bynum's *Holy Feast and Holy Fast*, she discusses body and food. She states that "our modern assumptions obscure the fact that food is food and body is body . . . our modern use of food and body as symbols of all that we seek to control seems to me a vain effort to hide from ourselves the fact that our control is not—and cannot be—total." If we look at the patterns of eating and dining in modern times and pay attention to Ms. Bynum's incisive research on medieval times, it doesn't take long to realize that the moderns have been busy trying to control body and food. But in this writer's opinion, the control has been in a subversive direction: instead of attempting to control (i.e., "care" about) what is being eaten, its naturalness and freshness, the pseudo-control has manifested itself by eating fat-free, cholesterol-free, taste-free, spirit-free, processed foods. This eating delusion has to do primarily with what is fashionable, and not so much with what may be preferable—a natural, hearty appetite—-the kind of appetite that doesn't compute calories but rather recognizes and desires abundant garden fresh flavors present in, for instance, those forgotten foot soldiers of food—soups and stews. In the late eighteenth century, an all-night taverner (Boulanger) started to sell soups, which he called "restoratives" or "restorantes." Boulanger is not only credited with siring the birth of the restaurant profession, his creativity with soups led to the spread of soups in France.

There's something intrinsically nourishing, when one is eating or drinking, about coating crusty bread in brothy or thick soup or stew filled with lentils, or rocket, or sausages, or spring onions with crispy noodles. Hearty soups and stews course through the body with a good glow that lasts for hours. Soup or stew any day, anytime, is the religious past and will be the religious future. In the near-distant past, numerous soup or stew choices were available on most menus, but they have been replaced with one choice of soup for the evening and no choice of stew. Few restaurants bother any more with the possible litany of soups or stews that are mini-gardens in a pot. People don't eat that way anymore. Or deep down, do they want to? Well, here's to those hearty souls who recognize Christian appetite in the not-so-religious present.

Cucumber Sambal Summer Soup
Serves Four

PEEL/CUBE   One large **cucumber**.

TOSS   Gently with 1 finely chopped, medium **red onion**, 1 **fresh serrano chile**, 1 cup split **green grapes**.

WHISK   One Tbs. **apple cider vinegar** into 1 Tbs. extra **virgin olive oil** with a dash of **sugar**, finely ground **sea salt**, and **cracked pepper**.

STIR   One-half cup **heavy cream** and 1–1/2 cups **skim milk** into oil emulsion and chill well.

ADD   Slowly 1–1/2 cups heavy cream. Stir, then chill well.

SERVE   In glass bowls with 1/2"-thick layer of freshly flaked coconut or toasted sesame. It's a summer soup that brings the tropical or subtropical mood of the Mexican Caribbean, North China Sea, or Indian Ocean into its artful perspective as I hypnotically stare at the sea.

COMMENT   Cream can be replaced with 1/2 orange stock, 1/2 freshly squeezed orange juice, and a lacing of fresh lime. Top with a spot of crème fraîche and lots of toasted sesame seeds. A plate of naan brushed with garlic ghee sets the soup in the direction of India.

Fiery Sausage and Olive Soup
Serves Four

REDUCE   Six cups **fruit stock** to 4 cups on high, fast heat, or simply mix 2 cups unsweetened **orange juice** and 2 cups unsweetened **apple juice** and simmer just to heat through.

SAUTÉ   One coarsely chopped, medium **red onion**, 2 minced medium **garlic cloves**, and 3 medium **hot chiles** of your choice in 3 Tbs. extra **virgin olive oil** until transparent. Stir in 1 cup pitted and crushed Greek or Italian **black olives** (or 1/4 cup olive paste) and cook on medium-high heat for 5 minutes.

ADD   One lb. **sweet Italian sausage** (removed from casing and pulled apart) to olive mixture, and flash-fry 5 minutes until crisp.

REMOVE   From heat and stir in 1 Tbs. finely minced **lemon zest**. Set aside.

SAUTÉ　　Eight Tbs. **bread crumbs** in 2 Tbs. extra virgin olive oil until evenly brown, taking care to keep redistributing bread crumbs with a rubber spatula to avoid burning.

SERVE UP　　Four deep bowls with equal portions of warm fruit broth or orange/apple liquid, add sausage/olive mix, sprinkle 2 Tbs. bread crumbs onto each bowl. If there happens to be some leftover tapenade (seasoned olive paste), dot the soup with it for that extra-intense taste lace.

COMMENT　　If fruit stock is not available, replace with 1/2 freshly squeezed or packaged unsweetened orange juice with apple juice (as mentioned above) or half white wine (sauvignon blanc/chardonnay), and reduce as in the first recipe step for fruit stock.

Orange-Buttermilk Corn Soup
Serves Six

BLEND/　　Two 6"-long-by-2"-wide pieces of **orange zest** strips
PROCESS　　with 1 cup **buttermilk** until orange zest becomes smooth with miniscule bits.

HUSK　　Eight ears of white or yellow **corn**, removing the ker-\nels with a sharp knife and cutting as close to the milky core as possible, or use two 16-oz. packages of thawed frozen corn.

REDUCE　　Six cups **orange stock** to 4 cups on high, fast heat. Taste for smooth, even flavor.

STIR　　Fresh corn kernels into reduced orange stock and simmer on medium heat for 10 minutes or until corn is al dente, firmly soft. Or, stir frozen corn into orange broth and cook for 5 to 6 minutes on high, fast heat.

WHISK IN　　Orange buttermilk plus 2 more cups of plain buttermilk, and cook on low heat for 15 minutes, stirring all the while for smoothness. Add 1 tsp. **cracked pepper** to taste.

PLACE　　In bowls and drop flat, leafy Italian parsley over the soup. Of all things that go well with buttermilky corn soup, a crumbly currant or raisin scone is it, or the impossible to find but delightful Hopi paper bread, piki, which is blue corn-meal flour rolled into sheets on a hot rock until wafer thin. When next in northern Arizona, seek out piki for a special Native American treat.

Orange-Tomato Lamb Stew
Serves Four

SAUTÉ Three crushed large **garlic cloves** and 1 pound **lamb** cut into 1/2" pieces in 2 Tbs. extra **virgin olive oil** on high, fast heat, stirring continuously until browned.

MIX In 1 pound coarsely chopped **roma tomatoes** or one 16-oz. package of Pomi brand chopped tomatoes (my preference), 3 cups freshly squeezed **orange juice**, 2 tsp. **allspice**, 1 tsp. **cinnamon**, 1 tsp. ground **sea salt** (regular salt will work also), dash **cracked pepper**, and begin simmering on low heat.

STIR In 1/2 lb. peeled **pearl onions** or 1 lb. coarsely chopped medium onions (approximately 2), and continue simmering for 45 minutes or until lamb is tender.

OPTIONAL Toss in 1 cup already-steamed **baby carrots** to draw tomato acid. Add 1/2 cup ground, sun-dried, oil-free **tomatoes** in addition to fresh or Pomi tomatoes used. One petite minced **chile** along with the orange and tomato converts this stew to Sicilian Stiphado, as it may have been originally before the Greeks made their way over to the island paradise of Sicily.

SERVE With Greek sesame bread and sit back, get tough, and have a piney glass of retsina with this stew. It's a great unpretentious Greek wine that never improves with age and keeps Greek people politicizing at the *plaka* about their ancient history and mythology.

COMMENT Have plenty of extra minced orange zest available to float on top. This is my version of the Greek specialty Stiphado—Lamb Stew with Pearl Onions. Stiphado sandwiches are far more messy and tasty sandwiches to feed children than the slop of Joe's.

Roasted Eggplant Mozzarella Soup
Serves Four to Six

REDUCE Eight cups mild **fruit stock** to 6 cups on high, fast heat.

QUARTER One 1 to 1–1/2 lb. **eggplant**.

ROAST In pan, no oil, along with 6 large whole cloves of **garlic** at 425 degrees Fahrenheit for 30 minutes or until eggplant surface is crusty brown and insides are soft and pulpy. Remove **eggplant stems**, pull meat from skins, coarsely mash or blend-process eggplant with roasted garlic, making a thick purée.

HAVE

Reduced **fruit stock** on high simmer. Add eggplant/garlic purée, stirring through. Remove from heat.

PLACE

Soup in heatproof bowls with **mozzarella** covering and, if possible, one other Italian cheese such as cacciocavallo or fontinella for added sharpness. Broil until cheeses crust into soup.

SERVE

With a basket of grissini, broken into bits and dropped into this poor man's caviar soup for that crunch-then-meltaway edge.

Scallop Celeriac Peanut Stew
Serves Four to Six

RINSE/PEEL/ ROAST

One quartered **celeriac (celery root)** at 425 degrees Fahrenheit (no oil) for 45 minutes until fork slides in and out easily.

ROAST

Six whole large **garlic cloves** (with chaff) at the same time until oozing. Remove chaff from garlic and fork-mash in bowl or blend-process with 1/4 tsp. ground **sea salt**, and 1/4 tsp. **cracked pepper** until puréed.

REDUCE

Six cups **fruit stock** to 4 cups on high, fast heat.

REMOVE

Pits from 2 small **peaches**, **stems** from 2 large **roma tomatoes**, and chop finely.

SAUTÉ

One lb. petite **bay scallops** in 1 tsp. **butter** and 1 tsp. **olive oil** on high heat for 4 to 5 minutes until scallop juices run milky and scallops are tender. Remove with slotted spoon.

ROAST/CHOP

One cup **unsalted peanuts**.

STIR TOGETHER

Scallops, celeriac/garlic, peaches, tomatoes into fruit stock, and heat through on medium heat 3 to 5 minutes. Place into wide shallow bowls with 1 Tbs. peanuts, and if any sun-dried, oil-free tomato chips are hidden away in the cupboard, toss a few into this potagey, autumnal soup.

Soups and Stews

Sherried Shiitake Soup
Serves Four

REDUCE Six cups **mild fruit** stock to 3 cups on high, fast heat.

ADD One cup good, dry **sherry**, and the **juice** of 1/2 **lemon**. Simmer on medium heat 5 minutes.

STIR In 1/2 lb. **shiitake** (or crimini) **mushrooms**, cut into dime cubes, and cook on medium heat for 10 minutes.

MINCE Finely 1 **roma tomato**.

LADLE Into four bowls, distributing mushrooms equally in each. Top with 1 Tbs. crème fraîche or yoghurt, minced tomato, 1 slivered scallion, 1 tsp. finely minced orange zest, and broiled walnut pieces. Have a few peeled spears of cucumber and radishes nearby with a saucer of cracked pepper for coating. Warm brioche wouldn't be too bad either.

COMMENT If fruit stock is not available, replace with freshly squeezed or packaged unsweetened orange juice, and instead of reducing orange juice, simply add sherry and lemon juice and continue from there.

Singed Onion Soup
Serves Four

FOLLOW Instructions for **singed onions** for 4 in Chapter 5.

REDUCE Six cups fruit stock to 4 on high, fast heat.

SAUTÉ Three crushed **garlic cloves** and 3 cups coarsely chopped **tomatoes** in **singed onion oil** on high heat for 5 minutes.

ADD One cup **sauvignon blanc** or similar white wine, and simmer on low for 10 minutes. Then add 4 cups reduced **fruit stock**, continue simmering on low for 15 minutes or until flavor has deepened.

REMOVE From heat. Stir through 2 Tbs. **butter**, 1 Tbs. **balsamic vinegar**, dash of ground **sea salt**, and 1 tsp. minced **orange zest**.

SWIRL One-half cup singed onions throughout each bowl, and serve with walnut rusks and a chunk of creamy goat cheese or whatever moves you. Sunday Night Chase-Away-the-Blues Soup.

Tomatillo Tomato Tortilla Soup
Serves Four

REDUCE

Eight cups **fruit stock** to 6 cups on high, fast heat.

REMOVE

Chaff and stems from 1/2 lb. **tomatillos** and 1/2 lb. (about 2 large) **roma tomatoes** or 3 regular tomatoes, and puree until smooth. Sauté 3 cloves minced **garlic** and 1 minced small **red onion** in 2 Tbs. extra **virgin olive oil** until crisp.

ADD

Tomatillos, tomatoes, garlic, and onions to reduced fruit stock, and simmer on high (not boiling) heat for 15 minutes. Stir in 1 Tbs. orange marmalade or jam of your choice to adjust flavor. If too tart, add more marmalade or jam.

STIR IN

Two tsp. freshly ground **cumin seed**, 1/2 teaspoon ground **salt**, and 1 to 2 minced **chiles** of your choice. Resimmer on high heat for 5 minutes.

TRANSFER

To bowls; drop numerous tortilla chips into each bowl. Drizzle a meager float of heavy cream over chips. If feeling adventurous or Oaxacan, grate a bit of dark bittersweet chocolate or Mexican chocolate (Ibarra) over the cream. A few steamy white corn tortillas and chipotles (smoked jalapeños) that have been softened in freshly squeezed warm orange juice will further enhance the Latino who is heating up this soup.

COMMENT

It wouldn't hurt to have some sabrosa Salsa Jacquelina available as an alternate choice to chocolate or, going one step further, try shaving a bit of chocolate into the salsa . . . not interested?

TONGUE TOUCHERS:
ENRAGED SUPPERS AND OTHERWISE

Wish I had time for just one more bowl of chili.
> —alleged dying words of Kit Carson

Slow, creeping heat. Lingering heat. Fast and dissipating heat. Explosive, scorching heat.

Vitamin Chile Heat. Healthy and hissing heat. Could this be risky eating or fear of seemingly risky foods? Chiles have been making their way into the American mainstream for sometime with steady, quiet tenacity. New chile-eaters/aficionados are popping up all the time . . . and with good reason. The brilliance of chile pain burns, exhilarates, and then cleverly prepares the eater for yet the next level of chile tolerance with swift and unrelenting beads of perspiration. Keep that icy pitcher of milk close by to begin the simmering down of chile tongues while continuing to feel the heat.

Cupping chili and supping chile should be at least a twice-weekly eating habit; this has proved itself in the evidence of flourishing Mexican restaurants. Chiles are not, however, restricted to any one ethnic group; they are hot pods malleable with numerous foods. To include a weekly enraged supper in one's eating habits is to encourage purge. After all, we are these human factories, busy with eating and "would-be" processing that often ends in non-processing. Fresh chile and fruit are natural purgatives that end that malfunction in a swift and cleansing way. I don't know about you, but this cook/human has a fondness for fruit-fire purgatory because of its very physical and seemingly spiritual purifying effects. So let's do the enraged deed, mix it all up, and start off this chapter with an unlikely kind of tongue toucher—my chilesque creation of Black Jaz Pickling Potion. *A los intrepidos, el mundo!* The world belongs to the fearless.

Black Jaz Pickling Potion
Five to Six Cups

MIX

Four cups **balsamic vinegar**, 3/4 cup **light brown sugar**, 6 peeled and fork-pierced medium **garlic cloves**, fresh **oregano** stripped from two 6" stems, 1/2 cup **black peppercorns**, 2 cups mashed fresh **raspberries** or 2 cups thawed raspberries pureed in 2 of the 4 cups of balsamic vinegar, fresh **rosemary** stripped from one 6" stem, 1 cup toasted **sesame seeds**, fresh **thyme** stripped from three 6" stems.

STORE

In airtight, preferably glass container in refrigerator or cool place for 30 to 90 days. When you think of it, stir thoroughly to redistribute ingredients.

PUREE

All ingredients smoothly in processor at end of 30-to-90-day storage period. Strain through cheesecloth or fine strainer, discarding solids. Some miniscule bits of peppercorns may remain in strained liquid. This is fine as they are the bold backbone to the Black Jaz sauce the liquid will eventually become.

PLACE

In sealed glass container, and refrigerate until ready to use.

SIMMER

One-half cup Black Jaz on medium-high heat, adding bits of **butter** during the sauce reduction. Taste, add more butter to tame the sauce, and continue this mellowing technique until Black Jaz reaches your comfort zone.

USE

Prudently in pastas, rices, soups, and stews; brush on poultry and seafood before broiling, grilling, and roasting.

COMMENT

Black Jaz sauce is provocative and bold in its color and flavor. Eat it gingerly, as it will be an entirely new taste sensation with some getting used to. If the eater can keep in mind that Black Jaz sauce is its own unique fruit-fire combo sauce, then he or she will develop/acquire the Black Jaz appetite, and if not, the cook replaces the black peppercorns with fresh or dried chiles of his or her choice.

Shortened Black Jaz
Five to Six Cups

MIX   All ingredients together in sealed glass container and let stand for 1 to 3 hours.

PUREE   In blender-processor until mixture is finely ground.

STRAIN   Through cheesecloth-lined strainer or fine strainer into large bowl, extracting as much liquid as possible. Transfer to glass container, and when ready to use,

REDUCE   One-half cup Black Jaz to 1/4 cup or more on medium simmer, depending on how much of the sauce you will need.

COMMENT   Be ready for this shortened version to be sharply potent. In the **REDUCE** step above, gradually add petite lumps of unsalted sweet butter and dashes of superfine sugar to achieve the balance of sweet to hot. The sugar should not be needed if a good quality balsamic vinegar is used.

Once again, the butter will mellow the sauce to where you want the flavor to be. If desirable and handy, toss in a few raspberries or split green grapes at the last minute before removing from the burner to freshen the Black Jaz one-two flavor punch.

Black Jaz Scallops with Black Sweet Rice
Serves Four

COMMENT

Black sweet rice can be purchased in Chinese/Asian grocery stores and is referred to as **red rice**, even though it cooks up a blackish red—a black-wine color, if you will. It is used widely in Victoria and Vancouver, British Columbia. It steams differently than normal rice, so monitor the cooking the first few times you work with this rice to determine what works well in your kitchen. It requires more water and a longer time to cook and does not fully absorb the water as white rice does. The flavor is similar to wild rice—nutty—minus the extra incurred cost of wild rice. If black rice is not available, do a mix of wild/white rice with appropriate water equivalent.

BRING

To boil 3 cups **water**, add 1 cup rinsed black rice, simmering 20 to 25 minutes until firmly soft, as in al dente with pasta. Water will not have been totally absorbed into rice, so taste rice grains for doneness. Rinse again and drain quickly with tepid water. Set aside.

REDUCE/ MELLOW

One-and-a-half cups of **Black Jaz liquid**, aged or shortened and strained, on medium heat in skillet with 2 Tbs. unsalted **sweet butter** until thickened, adding more butter to round out edges, if desired.

SAUTÉ

One pound petite **bay scallops** in 1 Tbs. unsalted, sweet butter and 1 Tbs. **olive oil** on high, fast heat for 3 to 5 minutes to retain their delicate tenderness. Strain scallops and return to pan; stir warm Black Jaz sauce throughout and remove from heat.

PLUNGE

Strained rice into warm water, quickly draining off water.

FLATTEN

Rice onto center of plate. Spoon Black Jaz Scallops over rice and surround outer edge of scallops and rice with 1 Tbs. darkly toasted **sesame seeds**. Scatter **blackberries** or **raspberries** or quartered **strawberries** here and there for the final color touch. A simple but knock-out 20-minute meal.

FURTHER COMMENT

Black Jaz Scallops is a fiery black-pepper dish with velocity and therefore needs a thirst-quencher with movement. So have a welcome icy pitcher of any sparkling water with freshly sliced lemons, limes, and oranges in it.

Chicken Wentletrap in the Thai Style
Serves Four

SIMMER
Three Tbs. **dark brown sugar**, 4 Tbs. juice from freshly squeezed limes, 1 cup mushroom soy sauce on medium heat for 15 minutes. Set aside.

POUND
Four skinned, split, boned **chicken breasts** with mallet until 1/8" thick. Roll breast lengthwise in the shape of a conical sea shell, i.e., wentletrap. Tie around shell shape from top edge to bottom edge with kitchen twine, allowing 1" spacing along the length of the rolled breasts.

MINCE
Finely 1 Tbs. **lime zest**.

JULIENNE
White portion of 1 **leek** into 5" strips. Set aside.

SAUTÉ
One peeled 5" **ginger stem** cut into pin-thin strips in 4 Tbs. extra **virgin olive oil** until dark brown. Gently remove from oil with slotted spoon and set aside.

ROAST
One-half cup **peanuts** golden brown, cool, and then chop finely.

STEAM COOK
Two cups **basmati rice** in 4 cups water until absorbed. Use black rice (sweet red rice) if available: follow cooking pattern in Black Jaz Scallops.

SEAR
Four tied chicken wentletraps in 1 Tbs. unsalted **sweet butter** and 1 Tbs. **sesame oil** in skillet on medium-high heat, turning with tongs until evenly browned. Place on tray in preheated 400-degree oven; roast 5 to 6 minutes until barely moist or juices run slightly pink when pierced. Remove chicken from oven, as juices will settle, and continue cooking chicken evenly.

FLASH-FRY
Four medium crushed **garlic cloves**, 2 fresh crushed Thai or 2 dried crushed **Thai peppers** (very small peppers, please, stems removed), 2 Tbs. raw minced **ginger** in 1 Tbs. unsalted sweet butter and 1 Tbs. **sesame oil** until browned. Add sugar/lime/mushroom soy sauce. Stir and reduce until there is body, i.e., the sauce hangs together. Remove from heat and toss in basil leaves and mint leaves stripped from 4 small stems each, then torn by hand into small pieces. Stir through sauce and remove from heat.

STEAM
Rapidly 24 snow peas 3 to 4 minutes until slightly firm. Remove from steamer and coat thoroughly with a touch of sesame oil for snow peas to glisten, set aside.

Enraged Suppers

STIR   Lime zest through drained basmati rice.

ASSEMBLE   By scooping rice onto center of plate, flatten with back side of serving spoon or rice paddle. Set chicken wentletrap onto center of rice. Cascade sugar/lime/soy/chile sauce onto chicken. Sprinkle roasted peanuts around outer edges of rice. Flank chicken with 6 snow peas, 3 on either side of the chicken. Feather julienned leek and fried ginger twigs on top of wentletrap.

COMMENT   This is a special dinner that requires time, so make it just that—special. The first time Chicken Wentletrap is tried, it will seem logistically difficult UNTIL you get the steps down, and then it will be a matter of just having a helper in the kitchen and perfecting the timing. This was the very labor-intensive standard item on the JazRanch menu that sent patrons to Thai heaven. Each of the many times I fired this dish on the cooking line, I was reminded of the Nana Restaurant in the Saudi Arabian quarter of Bangkok . . . a little like sitting in a smoky stew. All this requires for utter Thai fulfillment is an icy Lychee Sling alla Oriental Hotel in Bangkok, and if that is impossible, uncork some Singha beer. *Sawawasdee-ka! Sawawasdee-krup!*

**Crispy Noodle Nests
with Tomatillos and Prawns**
Serves Four

BOIL   Two quarts **water**. Break 1 lb. De Cecco brand dried **spaghetti** (not spaghettini or angel hair) in half, place half of the spaghetti in water, bringing back to the boil. Cover and turn off heat. Let stand for 25 to 30 minutes or until resistant to the bite, al dente. Cooked ramen noodles can replace the spaghetti. Allow 2 small packages for 4 people.

DRAIN   And cold-water plunge simultaneously. When spaghetti is totally water-free, divide and hand form into four nestlike piles and place on lightly oiled pizza or cookie tray. Keep nests separate . . . drizzle extra **virgin olive oil** lightly on surface of each.

PLACE   Under broiler and cook until spaghetti nests are browned on edges and the centers are soft, if possible. Use tongs to rotate nests while under the broiler to assure even crisping. Remove with stainless spatula and set aside.

SHELL/DEVEIN Thirty-two medium **prawns**, leaving tails on. Toss lightly with olive oil and broil quickly, 3 to 5 minutes total for both sides.

REMOVE Chaff from 1 lb. **tomatillos** and chop finely. Mix with 2 finely minced medium **garlic cloves**, 1/2 tsp. aromatized **cumin seeds** (heated in dry frying pan until slightly smoking) and then ground to a powder. Stir in 2 cups freshly squeezed **orange juice**. Taste for sweet to tart balance.

SIMMER Ten minutes on high, fast heat. Remove from burner.

ARRANGE Noodle nest in center of plate. Drizzle a bit of tomatillo/orange liquid onto the nests. Encircle each with 8 broiled prawns. Spoon chunky orange tomatillo bits on nests. Crack a high quality **black pepper**, such as Ponape, generously over noodles, prawns, and sauce.

COMMENT These crispy noodles are most adaptable. Use leftover spaghetti and quick-broil to serve with fresh tomatoes, singed onions, melted cheeses, or, after broiling, float on soup or chili. Use humble ramen noodles when 25 minutes is too much time to spend. Try placing tomatoes, onions, etc., under the crispy noodles and then a sauce on top with grated cheeses. Then rebroil momentarily until cheese is melted. Difficult finger food . . . with finger-licking goodness.

Curry (wet)
Serves Four to Six

AROMATIZE That is, heat up dry, oil-free heavy skillet until hot; you will know by the vapors when skillet is just about ready to smoke. Toss in the following:

1 tsp. whole **fenugreek**
1 tsp. whole **coriander**
1 tsp. whole **decorticated cardamon**
1 tsp. whole **cumin seeds**

Shake and slide the skillet constantly back and forth over heat until spices begin to smoke and release their fragrances/oils, i.e., aromatized. Immediately grind spices very fine in coffee grinder; it's okay to use the grinder as it leaves a lovely flavor for future coffee grounds.

MIX These spices with the following in a glass bowl:

3 new, firm **jalapeños**, finely chopped
1/2 cup **fresh green ginger**, peeled and finely
chopped
3 medium **garlic cloves**, finely chopped
2 tsp. grated **lemon rind**
1 tsp. **garam masala** (available in Indian spice
stores)
1 Tbs. white portion of **leek**, finely minced

ADD

To all ingredients above 1/2 cup extra **virgin olive oil**
and 1/4 cup **sesame oil**. What should more accurately
be used here is **ghee**, clarified butter, the East Indian
answer to butter. It is long-lasting stuff, like, made and
left to hang in the desert because of its built-in, natural
shelf life. If ghee is available, use it unless you are
avoiding saturated animal fats.

STIR

Curry and place in airtight jar in cool place for future
use, not necessarily the refrigerator as this congeals
the olive oil. Lasts indefinitely. Use for fruit, veggie,
chicken, lamb, and seafood curries.

COMMENT

Every now and then, this cook enjoys explosive heat,
so taste tester, proceed with curry caution, and have
plain naan bread or chapati to soak up flavors along
with fresh watermelon juice or mango juice to perhaps temper the tongue.

Fruited Garlic Pasta with Walnuts
Serves Two

BOIL

Two quarts **water** and add 1/2 lb. of fresh **tagliatelle**.
Bring to boil and turn off heat. Cover and let finish
cooking 4 to 5 minutes. If boxed tagliatelle is used,
follow through turning off heat, or be Italian and use
shells or rotini pasta. Cover and let finish cooking 20
to 25 minutes.

CUT

Away skin and pith from 1 **tangelo** (or orange).
Remove stem end of **tomato**, and cut tangelo and
tomato into small pieces.

MINCE

Finely 2 medium **garlic cloves**.

BROIL

One-half cup whole or halved **walnuts** until dark. Cool
and chop coarsely. Mix in bowl with 3 Tbs. grated
Asiago or **Parmesan cheese**.

BEGIN

Cooking 2 cups puréed/strained fruit stock (or freshly
squeezed orange juice) on high, fast heat, stirring in

garlic, tangelo, and tomatoes. Add 1 Tbs. unsalted **sweet butter**, simmering until reduced to 1–1/2 cups.

DRAIN   Pasta thoroughly; no excess water please.

PLACE   Pasta in skillet with fruited garlic sauce, and coat by using tongs to mix. Serve in bowls and drizzle a scant amount of extra virgin olive oil around edge of tagliatelle. Spoon walnut Asiago or walnut Parmesan cheese on pasta. Have some walnut pepper bread to swipe sauce from bowls.

Fruited Smoked Chicken and Chile Fettucine
Serves Four

REDUCE   Six cups **fruit stock** to 3 cups on high, fast heat. Add 1 cup **sauvignon blanc** and continue to simmer for 15 minutes. Remove and set aside.

SMOKE   In barbecue if possible, 4 deboned split, skinned **chicken breasts** until cooked/smoked. In the alternative, mix 1/4 tsp. **liquid smoke** with 1 Tbs. extra **virgin olive oil**, brushing on skinned chicken breasts. Broil 2 to 3 minutes on each side until barely moist. Remove and slice into thin strips.

REMOVE   Outermost stem end of 1 bunch **scallions** and mince finely along with 2 small **serrano chiles** or 1 medium serrano. Mix together.

COOK   One lb. dried **fettucine** al dente (i.e., bring water to boil; put fettucine in water and bring back to the boil; turn heat off; cover and check back in 10 to 15 minutes for perfect pasta and conserved gas or electricity). Dried pasta takes 20 to 25 minutes. Fresh fettucine takes 3 to 5 minutes.

WHILE   Fettucine is cooking, return reduced stock to burner and bring to simmer on medium-high heat. Rapidly whisk in 1/2 cup **heavy cream** and continue whisking until sauce begins to thicken moderately. Remove from heat. Stir in chicken strips, scallions, serranos.

STRAIN   Fettucine thoroughly and mix into chile/fruit-stock cream evenly. If need be, return fettucine in fruit-stock cream to burner to briefly rewarm.

MOUND   Fettucine on plates with chicken strips on top. Scatter singed ginger twigs or chips on top or 1 Tbs. finely minced lemon zest and palmfuls of freshly grated cheese. This is my offering plate on *I Morti* (Italian Day of the Dead) to keep their souls unleashed and dancing for more.

Pizzette D'Amici
Serves Four to Six

COMMENT

I could provide you with a pizzette formula that would be paper thin in texture and would be hours thick in preparation. So I suggest purchasing a box of that hot-roll mix that will get you to dinner in a less time-consuming manner.

FOLLOW

Box instructions for 1 **pizza crust**, rolled to your preference.

SAUTÉ

One finely chopped **red onion** in 2 Tbs. extra **virgin olive oil** until transparent. Add 1 lb. chopped **roma tomatoes** or 12-oz.-brand Pomi crushed tomatoes, 1/2 tsp. **superfine sugar**, 1/2 tsp. **cracked black pepper**, and cook on medium heat to a lumpy stew. Reduce this sauce until moderately thick for ladling onto the pizzette, about 10 minutes. Brush evenly with 2 Tbs. olive oil to seal dough. Spread tomato essence on uncooked pizza dough. Scatter 2 stems stripped and chopped **Italian parsley**, 1 stem stripped and chopped fresh **oregano**. Sprinkle 2 Tbs. **Asiago** or **Parmesan cheese** and 2 tsp. finely minced **orange zest** on pizza. Bake according to instructions; to intensify flavor quickly, I prefer to bake at 400 degrees Fahrenheit for 20 to 25 minutes.

WHILE

Pizzette is baking, make a batch of **singed garlic chips** from Chapter 5 page 48.

REMOVE

Pizza from oven, cutting whichever way you'd like. Drop singed garlic chips on each wedge or piece.

COMMENT

I do enjoy converting this to a salad pizza; that is, I toss a salad with a fruited vinaigrette or mustard and smother the pizza with greens and a last chasing of grated cheese with crushed dried red chiles. A pizzette to be shared with friends and fingers—Pizzette D'Amici—and drunk wide-eyed with a dry white Italian wine, maybe Vernaccia di San Gimignano (Toscana) or an always-delicious Piedmontese Gavi.

Utah Lamb, Pear, Date, and Toasted Bread Salad
Serves Four

TOAST

In preheated 400-degree oven, 2"-by-2"-square **sourdough bread cubes** (four 1" thick crusty Pacific Bay sourdough bread slices) until golden brown, using no oil. Keep turning cubes with tongs to ensure even toasting.

SAUTÉ

One lb. Utah or domestic **lamb stew** cut into 1"-by-1" pieces, 1 coarsely chopped medium **red onion**, 2 finely minced medium **garlic cloves** in 2 Tbs. unsalted **sweet butter** and 2 Tbs. extra **virgin olive oil** on medium heat until browned. Add 3 cups reduced **fruit stock**, 1 cup freshly squeezed **orange juice**, and simmer on low heat for 45 minutes to 1 hour until fruit/orange stock is absorbed and lamb is tender when pierced with a fork. Remove with slotted spoon, reserving juices for salad.

TOSS

One cored, coarsely cubed, slightly firm **pear** of your choice with 1/2 cup pitted/split **medjhool dates** with warm lamb, 1 Tbs. extra **virgin olive oil**, and lastly, gently, toasted sourdough bread cubes.

PLACE

Lamb salad in center of plate, drizzling sauce juices onto salad. Add spoonfuls of homemade yoghurt (or Nancy's yoghurt), and crack a bit of sea salt and black pepper on top. Drink some vino such as Rapitala Rosso from Sicily with its cherry top notes and most modest price—is there an '85 out there?

Sneakers and Gewürztramin Solitary Meals

SNEAKERS AND GEWÜRZTRAMINER: SOLITARY MEALS

And now I taste it again.
The meat of memory.
The meat of no change.
I raise my fork and I eat.
                    –Mark Strand

The symbolic sneakers have been kicked off, ending another long, productive or perhaps unproductive day. The house is empty. None of the familiar fellow human sounds are heard. A welcoming stillness encourages quiet, contemplative time for yourself. Pour a glass of cold gewürztraminer, German internal-motion wine. Rest those weary puppies as you spend precious moments reflecting on life, its ups and downs, its all arounds. Don't be seduced into turning on the vacant television or stereo for background companions. Get comfortable with this temporary solitude; use it to weave form and substance into your life, those threads that nebulous relationships prevent one from having. Be grateful. Think about family, good friends, good luck, food . . . food? At a time like this? Why fuss with cooking for just one tired, hungry human?

The year is 1996. The rules have changed. If you can't take the time to nourish yourself, how will you nourish others? Many of us seem not to care about nurturing each other with lovingly prepared food, but rather, ersatz food. Sunday evenings were once that special cocoonlike time that Americans reinforced the individual/group value of quiet, relaxed social eating at home.

Utah Mormons continue to practice this connective ritual within the context of their faith, calling it "Family Home Evening." Admittedly, this involves total family participation, but the act itself cements a useful, introspective habit of sharing with others as well as with just oneself. I cannot think of a better way to respect and stir the senses than to prepare a solitary meal for oneself whenever the occasion, rare or frequent, presents itself.

Make an impromptu meal by yourself, for yourself, to be enjoyed with yourself. Be aware of the kitchen sounds surrounding your cooking activity. Crushing the garlic, cutting the sweet red peppers, squeezing the oranges, chopping the walnuts. Feel the smooth stickiness of Gorgonzola Dolce cheese as you break it apart with your fingers. Watch the warm steam rise from the linguine. Don't touch that kitchen fan! Let the fragrant vapors wend their way through the house.

Sip wine. Pay close attention to your actions while cooking your solitary supper. Slow time down, for to try to do so is heroic. Whether the meal is a sandwich filled with thickly cut and broiled potato chips, and then soused with malt vinegar, or a peasant platter of crispy cauliflower stracinati with orange oregano focaccia, gravitate to the real thing—get to really know you—and that will in turn help to know, understand, and nourish others. Solitary cooking gives one no choice but to be conscious of one's own being/presence in a nonjudgmental manner, not to speak of eating the delicious end result. So, eat, drink, and contemplate no more; your fellow humans rap eagerly on the door.

Avocado/Lime/Chile Sandwich (or Guacamole Sandwich)
Serves One

FORK-MASH

Coarsely 1 small ripe Hass (dimpled, black-skinned) **avocado** with 1/4 tsp. **superfine sugar**, 1 small minced **serrano chile** or **fresh red jalapeño chile** (seeds removed), and freshly squeezed juice of 1/2 **lime**.

TOAST OR BROIL

One-half-inch-thick authentic **sourdough bread**, such as Pacific Bay San Francisco Style, on both sides. Spread coarse mash on toast. There will be plenty left for seconds or leftovers. Drink a Brazilian batida along with this up-tempo version of a sailor's butter sandwich, and plan on being nicely immobile for the afternoon or evening. *Joya!*

COMMENT

Be sure to make this a chunky avocado mash as this texture is comparable to eating a chunky salsa versus a smooth salsa. If you prefer smoother, then go all the way and blend to a buttery level. Use very thin toast such as Pepperidge Farm, spreading the avocado butter onto the bread, top with onion sprouts, and you now have what I have fed to my exhausted actors and dancers after rehearsals: guacamole sandwiches. Makes for hot feet, cool jazz.

Cauliflower Stracinati
Serves One

MINCE OR PROCESS

Six large **cauliflowerets** and 2 small cloves of **garlic** finely.

SAUTÉ

In 2 Tbs. extra **virgin olive oil** on medium-high heat until crisp. Keep tossing and pressing stracinati (cauliflower/garlic) into skillet.

PLACE

A wedge of toasted **focaccia bread** laden with 1 **fresh** stripped stem of **oregano**, 1 Tbs. extra **virgin olive oil** and the freshly squeezed juice of 1/2 **orange** or more, if your prefer. Flatten stracinati between focaccia toast slices, and if a **tomato** and **kiwi** are handy, chop coarsely onto the cauliflower mix. A good, old-fashioned, cellar red wine from the cantina will hit the spot.

COMMENT

Stracinati is Italian for "pulled." But the mincing or fine blending of the flowerets produce the same effect. This dish converts non-cauliflower eaters.

Date Onion Spread
Serves One Plus

SAUTÉ   One-half minced **red onion** in 2 tsp. extra **virgin olive oil** on medium heat until transparent.

ADD   Four **dates** and toss through onions for 2 to 3 minutes. Stir in 1/2 cup reduced **fruit stock** or unsweetened **orange juice**, and cook until dates/onions have totally absorbed juices. Cool and puree smoothly.

SPREAD   On **egg/onion matzo crackers**. Feeling feisty? Top your matzo meal with 1 very, very careful and miniscule bite into a **habañero chile** (scotch bonnet variety). Your true identity will now surface. Chase with very cold milk, if necessary.

USE   As a condiment with veggies, chicken, lamb, mountain meat loaf, or toss through couscous or Italian pastina.

Green Grape/Yoghurt Chicken Spiedini
Serves One

CUT   Two boned, skinless **chicken breasts** into 1" pieces, and place in small bowl. Cover with plain unflavored **yoghurt** and let soak up tartness for 30 minutes.

CUBE   Two 2" pieces of French or Italian **bread**, ending up with two 2" bread cubes coated with 1/2 tsp. finely minced **garlic** and **olive oil**.

THREAD   Yoghurt chicken pieces onto bamboo skewers, leaving space at either end for a bread cube. Crack pepper onto yoghurt chicken.

BROIL   On tray for 5 to 6 minutes, rotating skewer to evenly broil. When chicken is halfway done, place bread cubes at either end and continue rotating until chicken and bread are browned.

SPLIT   A handful of mixed **green**-and-**red seedless grapes**.

STRIP   One small **rosemary stem** of its leaves.

SET   Skewer on plate with split grapes; scatter rosemary on top, finishing with a bare drizzle of **honey**. Fancy chicken spiedini up or down with white or wheat toast points. This chapter should have been called "Sneakers, Spiedini, and Gewürztraminer."

75

Grilled Chicken/Wild Mushroom/ Roasted Garlic Sandwich
Serves One

ROAST

Two medium **garlic** cloves with chaff (or if so inclined, the whole head of garlic, for future use) on tray in preheated 400-degree oven until soft, 5 to 10 minutes. Remove, cool, and press roasted garlic mass through chaff.

SAUTÉ

One sliced **shiitake mushroom** (stem removed) with roasted garlic on high, fast heat until mushroom edges are singed brown. Add 1/4 cup **white wine** (Robert Pepi sauvignon blanc is most reliable when cooking with or drinking) and simmer fast until mushroom and garlic have absorbed wine. Remove from heat.

DRIZZLE

Three Tbs. **orange juice** on 1 skin-on, boned **chicken breast**.

GRILL OR BROIL

Until edges are crisp and juices run blond. Remove from heat. Cool and remove skin. Slice into strips.

SET

Chicken on a **dark bread** such as rogenbrot or just a simple polygrain **bread**. Spoon shiitake/garlic mixture onto chicken. Compress top bread slice into sandwich. Don't bother to cut it in half; just eat along with very small **tomatillos** or thinly sliced circlets of sun-dried tomatoes—the culprits of unstoppable nibbling.

Hearts of Caesar Salad Sandwich with Roasted Orange Tomatoes
Serves One

REMOVE

Outer leaves of 1 medium head **romaine lettuce**. Use only whitish green inner hearts of romaine. Gently remove core with hands, not knife. Set hearts aside.

SPLIT

One medium **tomato**, drizzling extra **virgin olive oil** and 1 tsp. finely minced **orange zest** on its surface.

BROIL

Until tomato is soft and oozing juices. Remove from oven and set aside to cool. Mash with fork. Set aside.

FORK-MASH

One high-quality **anchovy filet** in wooden bowl (preferably)—ceramic or glass will work otherwise. Add 1 tsp. **worcestershire sauce** and a pinch of powdered **cloves**, blending lightly but thoroughly into mashed anchovy. In separate bowl, whisk gently 3 Tbs. extra **virgin olive oil**, freshly squeezed juice of 1/2 **lime**, 1/2 tsp. finely minced **garlic**, dash of **superfine sugar**, mixing olive oil emulsion into anchovy emulsion, and stirring completely.

SET Hearts of romaine into wooden bowl with anchovy emulsion. Sprinkle 1 Tbs. of freshly grated **Asiago** or **Parmesan** over hearts. Gently and thoroughly coat hearts with Caesar sauce.

TOAST OR BROIL Two 1/2" slices of French, Italian, or *pain au levain* **bread** on both sides. Press orange tomato onto each toast slice. Mound coated hearts on toast until cumbersome but nonetheless inviting.

COMMENT Instead of using toast-toast, I have cut a wedge-shaped piece from a flat bread round, pressed opened the wedge, removed the dough, stuffing the orange tomato and Caesar hearts into the bread cavity. In either instance, hungry, lusting piglet sounds can be heard. Add more clove than suggested if you like this flavor as much as I do.

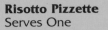

Risotto Pizzette
Serves One

BUY One 8-oz. Boboli Italian **bread-shell** package (original crust), containing two 4-oz. shells. Use one 4-oz. shell for the pizzette.

SAUTÉ One minced medium **serrano chile**, 1/2 minced **red onion** and 1/2 cup **risotto** (Italian rice—Arborio or Beretta brand) in 2 Tbs. **olive oil** and 2 Tbs. unsalted **sweet butter** until rice is browning evenly. Add 1/4 cup **white wine** and 1/4 cup freshly squeezed **orange juice**; begin simmering rice on medium heat. Thoroughly mix in 4 oz. crushed **Pomi tomatoes**, 1/8 tsp. **allspice** and **cinnamon**, and a dash of ground **cloves**. With risotto, it is wise to observe how the grains are cooking or not cooking; in which event, add more orange juice, crushed tomatoes, or fruit stock to barely cover the surface of risotto yet provide additional liquid for it to plump. Keep cooking and tasting for doneness with the goal being creamy risotto. Do not leave the stove. Keep wine handy while riding the risotto range. Cool rice for 10 minutes.

SPREAD Risotto on Boboli shell, edge to edge. There will be risotto left for breakfast. Top pizzette with 1 tsp. finely minced orange zest. Bake pizzette in preheated 400-degree oven for 15 minutes until crisp on edges. If desired, grate cheese over risotto.

BUNDLE UP And take this hot, stick-to-the-ribs pizzette and a pitcher of strawberry spumas outdoors. Eat and drink heartily, breathing in the calming effect of snow and sky, water and sky, and yet again, night sky. Keep the eyes peeled for illusory, hungry Navajo skinwalkers . . .

San Giuseppe Pasta Con Sarde
Serves One Plus Neighbors at the Door

BUY One small can of **Cuoco**; the already prepared, ready-to-go version of this unusual Milanese sauce is the easiest way of enjoying it. Once purchased, cooked, and tasted, it is hopeful that the cook will be interested in duplicating the ingredients in their fresh, untinned state. This is what is widely used by Italian Americans for Pasta Con Sarde on March 19, St. Joseph's Day.

BOIL One-half gallon **water**. Put in 1/2 lb. boxed De Cecco **perciatelli** (broken in half) and bring back to boil, uncovered. Turn off heat; cover, letting it self-cook for 20 to 25 minutes.

SAUTÉ One-half cup **bread crumbs** in 3 Tbs. **olive oil** until golden brown. This cooking should be done on medium heat with a wooden spoon, constantly stirring crumbs as they slowly brown. Try to avoid clumping and when it does occur, break up with spoon. Remove from heat, set aside.

SIMMER Contents of 1 small can pasta con sarde sauce (Cuoco brand).

DRAIN Pasta and stir sauce evenly through.

SERVE On plate, with generous topping of the sautéed bread crumbs. If cheese is absolutely needed because of habit, use sparingly. A Sicilian twist of the cheek and toast to the humble, happy recognition of food fit for St. Joseph and the rest of us—*A Cent Annos!*—One Hundred Years!

Wasatch Mountain Meat Loaf
Serves One Plus One

NOTE

Singed garlic chips are needed to incorporate into the following meat loaf, so head back to Chapter 5, page 48, for recipe to have ready.

MIX

One **egg** with 1/2 cup **bread crumbs**, 1/4 cup freshly grated **Asiago** or **Parmesan cheese**, 1 small stripped stem **oregano leaves** (fresh or dried), 1/2 tsp. finely minced **orange zest**.

ADD TO

One-quarter lb. **ground lamb** and 1/4 lb. **ground sirloin**, mixing thoroughly with hands. Then, drop 1/8 cup singed garlic chips into meat mass, working in evenly but lightly so as not to break the chips. Form into crudely shaped loaf and coat lightly with olive oil. Place in small loaf pan and bake in heated 400-degree oven for 15 to 20 minutes or until juices run pink/beige. Remove from oven and let settle; cool.

GRAB
AND SLAP

A plenty-thick slice of meat loaf between two slices of any bread—-yeah, go ahead, use the motel pillow white bread—and spurt on the Tabasco. Set a jar of sweet gherkin pickles on the ranch table and start swappin' stories. This meat loaf ain't so tough that yuh have to sharpen yore knife to cut the gravy, 'cause there ain't no gravy.

COMMENT

Just drizzle Tabasco on Wasatch Mountain Meat Loaf, minus any bread, wash it down with Mountain Dew . . . and you're ready to ride the nearby Oquirrh range, pardner.

Beginnings or Endings
Sweet Dreams

BEGINNINGS OR ENDINGS:
SWEET DREAMS

Add just a dusting of sugar, use your spoon to draw up a little coffee
and mix it with the foam. Now spoon up the frothy sweetened milk
between bites of brioche and relax.
–Tim Parks
Italian Neighbors

Italians have had an ongoing, comfortable relationship with velocity,
albeit a Ferrari or Fiat machine dream, sparkling wines, spumas, sparkling
waters. Their day begins with the morning cappuccino, an evening espresso
and corretto that can be drunk at anytime during the day. It's a built-in
motion-maintenance policy for an entire culture that additionally can relax
with the greatest of grace, daily uplifting and rejuvenating each other's
spirits. What a way to start, end, and share each day.

Interestingly enough, coffeehouses in America have evolved into
descendants of the diner and local neighborhood taverns. After home and
work, we have no place to go anymore that we trust, unlike the highly rit-
ualized cappuccino/espresso/la dolce vita in Italia. Although American
coffeehouses of the '90s lack the richness and ceremony that pervade
pasticcerias in Italy, we certainly have a starting base from which to sip.
Thank you, Starbucks, for the great sips; but what about the sweets? And,
further, what is good coffee without good dessert, and what is good
dessert without good coffee? The coffee issue is usually one that can be tip-
toed around in the minds of most folks. Well, I'm just not folksy. In fact, I
am the cappuccino macchiato curmudgeon. Barista, run the other way if
my cappuccino is not right and picture perfect . . . especially if the pastries
and biscotti are not even an edible possibility with A.M. cappuccino.

Such a dilemma, and for no reason at all. It appears that there is a per-
vasive movement to commit obscene little sugar murders in the form of
pastries and desserts. Whoever said "espresso takes many forms, but for
connoisseurs and cigar lovers, the dark brew is the pinnacle of coffee
enjoyment," pretty much summed up how this writer feels concerning her
desire for a true and tasty pinnacle to savor with her coffee. In my dreams.

The word "dessert" is a misnomer. It suggests—rather, it dictates to the
diner that a dessert is to be eaten at the end of a meal. Not so. If the word
"dessert" was changed to "sweets," and said sweets were reworked to open
a meal (open the palate) and/or close a meal (cleanse/close the palate), there
might be a renewed renaissance in the making of sweets. It is as though
sweets (alias desserts) have been reduced to army mess items. The term "just
desserts" seems to deliver the last swift blow—just desserts.

Take me to the Hayes Street Grill in San Francisco for the watermark
créme brûlée in America along with a good, rich, round cup of coffee—to
begin my meal. Take me to Al Tavolino in Milano for the simultaneously
scalding hot and icy-cold delectable sweet, called meneghina alla griglia, to
begin my meal. After all, the digestivi are available as curatives between
courses, and indigestion is not an issue. I have watched, then participated in,
the 10:00 A.M. very long queue outside a pizzeria in Orvieto, Italy, to eat a
delectable chile pizza for breakfast, starting with cappuccino. This was not a
dream. I was in Sweet Heat Heaven.

Beginning the day with sliced and sautéed crisp fresh jalapeños, serranos,
and ginger, then dipped in a mixture of honey and lime—wake-up food. Having
a mouthful of mountain mousse before a salad jump-starts the salivary glands
into la dolce vita . . . beginnings and/or endings of sweet with salty, tart with
sweet, hot with cold, and hot with sweet. Candied chiles. Dream food.

81

Banana Rice Pudding
Serves Four

BOIL

Three-fourths cup **water**. Add 1/2 cup **basmati rice**, or any rice will do. Simmer rice on medium-high heat for 10 minutes. Remove from heat and drain.

COMBINE

Partially cooked rice with 1 cup **whole milk** in covered saucepan for 30 minutes, stirring frequently, until grains are plump and firm. Remove from heat.

WHISK

Four **egg yolks** in a bowl with 1/3 cup **superfine sugar** and 1 Tbs. finely minced **orange zest**.

FORK-MASH

Coarsely 2 medium-ripe **bananas**. Squeeze juice of 1/2 **lime** on banana mash and blend with spatula or wooden spoon.

GRADUALLY

But steadily whisk egg-yolk mixture into milky rice in saucepan. Return to burner on low heat, stirring until creamy and thick. Remove from heat.

FOLD

Banana mash into rice. Allow to cool for 10 minutes and serve up in four bowls. Float **heavy cream** on each. Break **zwieback toast** or plain Jacquelina biscotti in pieces and sink into heavy cream.

or . . .

Serve rice pudding in one large bowl with four spoons. This is a communal pudding intended for kids and adults alike. No fighting over zwieback or biscotti.

Cafe Fortissimo
Makes One-and-three-fourths Cups

MEASURE

One cup **superfine sugar**, place in 12-oz. glass jar. Pour 10 oz. **moscato di grappa** of your choice over sugar. Seal jar and set in cool place overnight or for several days. When ready to use,

POUR

Four hot cups of French and Italian roast **coffee**, freshly ground. Add a teaspoon of the **grappa syrup** to each (be sure to shake grappa syrup well). If grappa is too strong, a **twist of lemon** rubbed around the edge of the cup will lessen the liquor load.

TASTE

And if more Cafe Fortissimo is desired, prepare to begin talking nonstop with *entusiasmo*. This coffee, along with fresh fruits, ricotta, and fennel rice cookies, will ensure the late departure of hard-core coffee and cookie devotees.

COMMENT This moscato di grappa will last for several coffee fortissimo sessions; it does well poured over sorbets and finished with a squeeze of lime.

Chocolate Souffle Cake

Serves Six to Eight

MELT Twelve oz. **dark unsweetened chocolate**, 5 oz. unsalted **sweet butter**, and 5 **egg yolks** in top portion of double boiler, stirring frequently to keep blended.

REMOVE From heat and gently fold 8 stiffly beaten **egg whites** into chocolate. Butter 9-inch springform pan, and pour chocolate mass into pan.

BAKE In preheated 375-degree oven for 20 minutes. Cake may appear cracked on surface, as in an earthquake cake. Allow to cool; refrigerate for later use. Be sure to remove from refrigerator at least 45 minutes before serving to allow flavors to surface.

SERVE With 3 oz. **fresh raspberries** pressed onto glass plate (or frozen raspberries, thawed and pureed). Rest cake on raspberries and top with **créme chantilly**, a heavy cream whipped with powdered sugar and vanilla.

Coffee with kirschwasser, coffee with cognac, or just coffee with chocolate souffle cake puts that "chocolate jones" in check for a few months.

COMMENT Chocolate Souffle Cake was baked daily for 2 years at JazRanch in Salt Lake City, altitude 4,500 Feet. At lower elevations, experiment with baking at 350 degrees for equivalent cake uniformity.

Fennel Rice Cookies
Makes About Three-Dozen Cookies

BLEND/ CREAM Two 4-oz. sticks unsalted **sweet butter**, 3/4 cup **powdered sugar**, 1 **egg yolk**.

ADD Two cups **rice flour**, 2 tsp. **baking powder**, 2 tsp. ground **cardamon**, 2 Tbs. whole **fennel seeds**, 2 Tbs. **orange** or **rose flower water**.

WORK Dough with hands until a solid, nonsticky mass, i.e., do not overwork. Place in plastic bag in refrigerator for 3 hours.

REMOVE From refrigerator. Knead gently for 10 minutes.

FORM Hazelnut-sized balls 2–1/2" apart on buttered and parchment-paper-lined cookie sheet. With underside of teaspoon, flatten slightly (make divot in cookie).

BAKE In preheated 350-degree oven on middle rack for 15 to 20 minutes. Because of rice flour, cookies will be white when done. Remove from oven and allow to totally cool. Take care when handling this Italian version of a delicate Iranian sweet, as it is fragile in the hand and meltaway in the mouth, thanks to Mr. Simonian's delicate touch. If it were possible, and this would be highly unlikely unless I were on a Greek Island, I would relish a perspiring, cold glass of sour cherry juice with *nan-e berenji*.

Layered Pumpkin Mincemeat Pie
Serves Eight

COMBINE One-and-a-half cups **all-purpose flour**, 1 Tbs. **super-fine sugar**, 8 Tbs. softened unsalted **sweet butter** in processor and pulse-blend into pea-sized granules.

ADD Juice of freshly squeezed medium **lime**, 1 Tbs. finely minced **lime zest**, 3 to 4 Tbs. **ice water**, blending until ball forms in processor. Remove dough, slightly flatten on plate, cover with tea towel, and rest one hour in refrigerator.

HAND PRESS Dough into 9" springform pan, building a high-shoul-dered crust up sides of pan, about 2" to 3" high to accommodate both layers. Rechill formed pie dough in refrigerator while preparing filling.

NOTE If you would prefer not cooking a whole **pumpkin**, pur-chase tinned pumpkin, using same amount as fresh.

QUARTER And cut 1–1/2 lb. fresh pumpkin in 1"-to-2" pieces (which should yield 4 cups roasted pumpkin).

ROAST In preheated 375-degree oven until pumpkin is scoopingly soft. Cool; remove skin, stringy pith, and seeds.

MASH-BLEND Pumpkin, adding 1/3 cup superfine sugar to smooth consistency. Gently, swiftly, but thoroughly stir 4 beaten **eggs** into pumpkin. If tinned pumpkin is used, beat sugar and eggs in accordingly.

PLACE
Two cups **mincemeat** (sold in glass jars) in mixing bowl, pouring 1 cup freshly squeezed **orange juice** or packaged, home-style, unsweetened orange juice over mincemeat, blending thoroughly with wooden spoon. Add 1 Tbs. freshly ground **cinnamon** (if possible) and 1/2 cup coarsely chopped **pecans**; stir throughout.

SPREAD
Mincemeat on bottom half of uncooked, chilled crust, taking care that there is no excess orange juice to make bottom of pie crust soggy. When all mincemeat is used, layer with roasted, creamy pumpkin mass.

BAKE
In preheated 350-degree oven for 1 hour or more until crust is dark brown. Cool on trivet for 45 minutes, then refrigerate for 45 minutes so that pumpkin and mincemeat set and pie can be cut without relative fear of high-shouldered crust crumbling.

THE STORY
On this sweet is simple. I got tired of making two separate pies to offer patrons during the holidays and wanted them to have both tastes at the same time in one bite. It is a winning sweet and should be served with the usual dollop of fresh heavy whipped cream and a pot of cafe filtre (French press) coffee, and eaten close to a cigar-friendly space for those who wish to light up a casual Frisco or Cohiba (this writer included) after the sated satisfaction of Layered Mincemeat Pumpkin Pie with Créme Fraîche.

COMMENT
I prefer to make my own mincemeat but understand that it can be labor intense. I have also reduced the amount of mincemeat by 1 cup and replaced it with fresh fall fruits, be it pears, persimmons, and sometimes even chestnuts.

MORE COMMENT
The eating image carved indelibly in my culinary memory is that of a close friend, Georgann Tucson. I awakened one early morning as her houseguest and meandered to the main house. There she stood in her crispy, waffly white robe with a white silk ribbon holding back her red locks, leaning against her stove, starting yet another day in life, eating leftover pumpkin-mincemeat pie that was swimming in cream, and smiling that toothsome, then tight-lipped smile of breakfast pleasure.

Mountain Mousse with Lemon Créme Fraîche
Serves Four to Six

Lemon Créme Fraîche
Two Cups

POUR
Two cups fresh **heavy cream**, 6 Tbs. **buttermilk**, 2 tsp. finely minced **lemon zest** into sealed glass container. Let stand in warmth for 36 hours, close to a stove pilot light and wrapped in a small wool throw—treat it tenderly.

STIR
Two-to-three times during creaming process. When full time has elapsed, refrigerate to achieve butter consistency, about 4 to 6 hours. This fresh cream lasts indefinitely and is far superior to sour cream.

BEAT
Two **eggs** and 1–1/3 cups **brown sugar** until blended. Mix 4 Tbs. **all-purpose flour**, 2–1/2 tsp. **baking powder**, and stir into egg/sugar mixture. Add 3/4 cup coarsely chopped **walnuts** and 3/4 cup peeled, chopped, **tart green apple**; blend gently and thoroughly.

BAKE
In preheated 350-degree oven for 30 to 35 minutes in buttered flat glass tart dish. This sweet comes out looking hilly, cavernous, rustic.

SCOOP
Servings with flat ice cream tool and top with lemon créme fraîche. This is a creation for my Cowboy/ Cowgirl patrons—food eaten with campfire coffee on the open range or in the high Uintahs. Serves two hungry Marlboro men or women or 4 to 6 ladies undesirous of crépe suzette tummies.

Pear and Muscovado Sugar Cake
Serves Six

NOTE
Muscovado is a specialty **sugar**. It is the darkest of brown in color and soft-to-powdery in texture. If it is not available, use the darkest of brown sugar.

CORE/PEEL
And cut 3 large ripe **d'anjou pears** into medium cubes.

STIR
Two Tbs. freshly squeezed **lime juice** and 2 Tbs. **pear brandy** through pears. Set aside.

COMBINE
Three-fourths cup all-purpose, pre-sifted **flour**, 6 Tbs. muscovado or dark brown sugar, 1/3 cup **buttermilk** until blended.

BEAT	Two **eggs**, stirring through flour mixture. Butter inside of 9" springform pan. Pour batter evenly into pan. Drop pears evenly over batter, pushing them just below the surface.
BAKE	In preheated 350-degree oven until cake is slightly firm, about 40 to 45 minutes. Cool and release from sides of pan.
or	Simply remove spoonfuls from the pan and enjoy as cake with whipped cream or cake pudding with cream. A saucer of whole walnuts sprinkled with muscovado or dark brown sugar and floating in pear eau de vie are pear cake taste-treat companions.

Pineapple Brownie
Serves Six

BUY	Six of your favorite 4"-by-4" **chocolate brownies**.
SKIN/CORE/ CHOP	One small-sized fresh **pineapple** coarsely.
PLACE	In mixing bowl and, depending on tartness of pineapple, stir 2 oz. **superfine sugar** through mixture. Test taste.
QUARTER	Brownies and gently mix evenly with pineapple.
DOT	One tsp. unsalted **sweet butter** on surface of 12"-to-14" round or square baking pan (glass preferred). Place pineapple brownies in pan and bake in preheated 350-degree oven for 20 minutes.
REMOVE	From oven. Spoon 1 cup **pine nuts** all across cooked concoction. Return to oven, placing under broiler and monitoring carefully until pine nuts are evenly toasted brown.
SERVE	This unpretentious gratin warm or chilled, with or without Canadian vanilla ice cream and pitchers of iced half-and-half pineapple/orange juice enlivened with sparkling water.

Sweet Dreams

Sleeping Milk Compote Cake
Serves Eight or Ten

CUT

Apricots and **pears** into thin short strips (medium julienne). Cover with 2 cups freshly squeezed **orange juice**. Add 1/4 cup **superfine sugar**, 1 tsp. freshly ground **nutmeg**, 1 tsp. freshly ground **cinnamon**, and 1/2 cup toasted, finely chopped **walnuts**. Blend well and let compote rest for 1 hour while preparing cake.

CREAM

Three-fourths cup **superfine sugar** with 1/2 cup unsalted **sweet butter** until smooth, mixing in 3 gently beaten **eggs**.

SIFT

Together 2 cups **all-purpose flour**, 1 tsp. **baking powder**, 1 tsp. **baking soda**. Slowly and evenly, add dry ingredients to creamed butter-and-egg mixture. Add 1 cup **yoghurt** and blend well.

STRAIN

Excess orange juice from apricot/pear compote and reserve juice. Stir compote through batter evenly.

PLACE

In buttered and floured 9" springform pan. Bake in preheated 350-degree oven for 55 minutes or until toothpick comes out clean. Cake should still be moist when done. Remove and cool.

SERVE

With additional heaps of yoghurt, preferably your own freshly made. As an alternative to fresh yoghurt, mix 1/2 cup sour cream with 1/2 cup yoghurt to produce similar texture and flavor of fresh yoghurt. Then drizzle reserved compote orange juice over cake.

SLEEPING
MILK

Is a term used by Czechoslovakians and Hungarians to identify freshly made yoghurt. Prepare for a most restorative nap after ingesting compote cake.

Sweet Heater
Makes One Fifth

HAVE Handy a clear or green fifth (750 ml) wine bottle for Sweet Heater ingredients.

PIT One medium **pear** of your choice and slice half of the pear into thin strips that will fit into the neck of the wine bottle; drop into the liquid.

DE-STEM Two large **strawberries** and do the same.

SKIN One **kiwi**, using half of it cut into pieces as above.

PEEL And thinly slice one 1"-by-1" piece **fresh ginger** as above.

SLIVER One **green serrano chile** and 1 **red jalapeño chile**.

DROP All ingredients into bottle, adding 2 tsp. **fennel seeds** and pour 2 1/2 cups **light corn syrup** or light-colored **honey** to top of bottle shoulders and/or bottom of gooseneck portion of bottle. Shove a cork halfway into bottle. Don't refrigerate but keep in a cool place. Shake the bottle every now and then to redistribute ingredients. Forget about Sweet Heater until you happen to remember it again. Should fermentation begin to occur, remove from bottle, blend, and strain; then use Sweet Heater quickly. A few bubbles here and there, however, are natural.

COMMENT Sweet Heaters are meant to include whatever is in the cupboard or refrigerator. This means the palette is endless. Replace fennel seeds with whole cumin seeds, or anise seeds, or toasted sesame seeds. This is a special sweet/hot syrup that can be used for most anything that is marinated, steamed, sautéed, roasted, broiled, or just poured straight out of the bottle onto your food. Sweet Heaters can be left to their own creative juices. The fruit will begin to release its juices into the syrup or honey, dispersing more fruit and then heat flavor, as well as thinning the syrup down. Hence, a small portion goes a long way, but because of its unique flavors, it gets eaten rapidly. My editor, Caroll, can attest to that. Do a series of custom Sweet Heaters and individualize each by painting or scrawling your name on each, giving them as gifts, or just hoarding a few to feast your eyes upon when the need presents itself.

Tortoni Jacquelina
One Quart (approximately)

COMBINE   One-half cup **water** and 1 cup **superfine sugar** in saucepan. Simmer on high heat until sugar syrup coats a wooden spoon.

WHISK   Four **egg yolks** with 1/4 teaspoon **salt** until very thick.

ADD   Sugar syrup in fine stream to egg emulsion gradually, continuing to whisk until thick and smooth. Chill.

STIR   Into chilled, sugared eggs: 1/4 cup **grappa**, 1 Tbs. Da Vinci **hazelnut flavoring**, along with 1 cup toasted and finely chopped **hazelnuts** with skins.

WHIP   Three cups **heavy cream**. Fold whipped cream into sugared eggs/grappa/hazelnut mixture.

PLACE   In a sealed container such as a bombe mold or, more practically, a one-quart, square plastic container, and freeze.

WHEN READY   To eat, use flat ice cream serving spoon and pile tortoni onto plate or bowl, adding more chopped hazelnuts. Do the deed: cascade Nutella over the tortoni—the stuff bambini eat in the morning upon awakening. Sweets for the Italiana or Italiano in your soul.

CHAPTER 10

INNOCENT PLEASURES
IN THE HIDDEN WEST

Sometimes we must look at things with innocence, gentleness . . .
But evening has fallen, unfortunately. Look, I even drank all the wine.
— C. P. Cavafy
"A Great Feast At The Home Of Sosibios"

The dark innocence of poets and their process is rich with the body of life and is its very soul. In "The Other Voice," Octavio Paz speaks "of our present and future life" as it relates to what he calls the circular process of the market (economy). He further states that ". . . the market is highly efficient, but it has no goal, its sole purpose is to produce more in order to consume more."

This is a welcome warning to the planet that I hope, along with Mr. Paz, is absorbed, and we come to our senses. It is time to stop and live with each other compassionately, not greedily.

Be genuinely concerned about our fellowman. Actually do random acts of kindness for strangers as well as friends. Cook each other modest and pleasurable meals of peaceful restoration: chile posole with anchovy pineapple mash; spaghetti with garlic, green grapes, red crushed chile peppers, tomatoes, and extra virgin olive oil; pasta with burnt butter, orange stock, and cheese swirled through. Do what the ancient poetry mirror does—reflect, confront, soothe, share. Good cooking, good food, and good humor with good friends should not have to be the struggle it has been for many. Cooking and sharing is the conduit to our inner social and spiritual selves. Take—No, demand and steal time to assemble these most basic essentials in life in order to begin the wind down leading to the renaissance and restoration of ourselves and each other. For, as Octavio Paz suggests, ". . . if human beings forget poetry, they will forget themselves, and return to original chaos." My choices were made long ago as a child and have remained constant. Natural passion. Innocent eating pleasures. Good mental health. *Il Primo Moture*. The driving spark within all humans. Rest and restore. Look, I even ate all my fruits and chiles . . .

BIBLIOGRAPHY

Andrews, Colman. *Catalan Cuisine.* New York: Collier Books/Macmillan Publishing Company, 1988.

Andrews, Colman. *Everything on the Table.* New York: Bantam Books, 1992.

Bynum Walker, Caroline. *Holy Feast and Holy Fast.* Berkeley and Los Angeles, California: University of California Press, 1987.

Conran, Terence & Caroline. *The Cook Book.* New York: Crown, 1980.

David, Elizabeth. *An Omelette and a Glass of Wine.* New York: Viking Penguin, 1985.

DeWitt, Dave, and Nancy Gerlach. *The Whole Chile Pepper Book.* New York: Little Brown & Company, 1990.

Grigson, Jane. *Jane Grigson's Fruit Book.* New York: Atheneum, 1991.

Grigson, Jane. *The Mushroom Feast.* Great Britain: Michael Joseph, 1975.

Hessayon, Dr. D.G. *The Fruit Expert.* Great Britain: Jarrold & Sons Ltd., 1993.

Leyel, Mrs. C.F., and Miss Olga Hartley. *The Gentle Art of Cookery.* London: Hogarth Press, 1925.

Ortiz, Elisabeth Lambert. *The Complete Book of Caribbean Cooking.* New York: M. Evans & Co., 1973.

Paz, Octavio. *The Other Voice.* New York: Harcourt Brace Jovanovich, 1991.

Rangarao, Shanti. *Good Food from India.* Bombay: Jaico Publishing, 1968.

Roden, Claudia. *A Book of Middle Eastern Food.* New York: Alfred A. Knopf, 1972.

Roden, Claudia. *Everything Tastes Better Outdoors.* New York: Alfred A. Knopf, 1984.

Santolini, Antonella. *Napoli in Bocca.* Palermo, Sicily: Edikronos, 1981.

Schiavelli, Vincent. *Sicilian Table.* New York: Carol Publishing Group, 1993.

Strand, Mark. *The Continuous Life.* New York: Alfred A. Knopf, 1992.

Suskind, Patrick. *Perfume.* New York: Alfred A. Knopf, 1986.

Tannahill, Reay. *Food in History.* New York: Stein and Day, 1973.

Thorne, John. *Outlaw Cook.* New York: North Point Press/Farrar Strauss Giroux, 1994.

Thorne, John. *Simple Cooking Food Letters.* Castine, Maine: Spring/Summer 1990.

Tropp, Barbara. *China Moon Cookbook.* New York: Workman Publishing, 1992.

Waters, Alice. *Chez Panisse Pasta & Calzone.* New York: Random House, 1984.

Wolfert, Paula. *Mediterranean Cooking.* New York: Times Books, 1977.

INDEX

A

Al Tavolino, 81
Alcoholic beverages. See Staples*: Wines/Beers/Spirits
Anchovy, 47, 76; pineapple mash, 92
Andrews, Colman, 53
Antipasto, 51
Appetizers: Chapter 5, 45–51. See also "High-Peasant Eats: Appetizers"
Apple: Apple or Dried Apple Vinaigrette, 32; Apple Mustard, 40; Smoked Trout Club Sandwich with Apple Horseradish, 50. See also Staples*: Apple juice
Apricot: Apricot or Dried Apricot Vinaigrette, 32
Arizona: Chinle, Hotevilla, Tuba City, 15; Northern, 55
Aromatize (technique), 67
Avocado/Lime/Chile Sandwich, 74
Axel, Gabriel (film producer), 21

B

Babette's Feast (film), 21
Balzac, 46
Banana: Banana Mustard, 40; Banana Rice Pudding, 82
Beans, variety of, 48
Beef: Wasatch Mountain Meat Loaf, 79
Beer. See Staples*: Wines/Beers/Spirits
"Beginnings or Endings: Sweet Dreams" (Chapter 9), 80–90; Banana Rice Pudding, 82; Cafe Fortissimo, 82–83; Chocolate Souffle Cake, 83; Fennel Rice Cookies, 83–84; Layered Pumpkin Mincemeat Pie, 84–85; Mountain Mousse with Lemon Crème Fraîche, 86; Pear and Muscovado Sugar Cake, 86–87; Pineapple Brownie, 87; Sleeping Milk Compote Cake, 88; Sweet Heater, 89; Tortoni Jacquelina, 90
Betty Blue (film), 21
Biscotti, 81
Black Jaz: Pickling Potion, 62; Shortened, 63; Scallops with Black Sweet Rice, 64
Boboli, 77–78
Bouillon, 9. See also Broth, Fruited;

"Fruited Fiery Broths"; "Fruited Fire in the Kitchen"
Boulanger, 53
Bread. See Staples*: Bread
Broth, Fruited, 26. See also "Fruited Fiery Broths"; "Fruited Fire in the Kitchen"
Brownie: Pineapple Brownie, 87
Butter. See Staples*: Butter
Buttermilk: White Vegetable Broilcakes, 51; Orange-Buttermilk Corn Soup, 55; Pear and Muscovado Sugar Cake, 86–87
Bynum, Caroline Walker (author), 53

C

Cafe Fortissimo, 82–83
Cake: Chocolate Souffle Cake, 83; Pear and Muscovado Sugar Cake, 86–87; Sleeping Milk Compote Cake, 88; Tortoni Jacquelina, 90
California: geography, 9; Berkeley, 11, 46; San Francisco, 31, 81
Calmyrna fig, 47
Capers, 48
Carson, Kit, 61
Cauliflower: White Vegetable Broilcakes, 51; Cauliflower Stracinati, 74
Cavafy, C. P. (poet), 47, 92
Celeriac (celery root): Scallop Celeriac Peanut Stew, 57
Chapati, 68
Cheese. See Staples*: Cheese
Cherry Radish Vinaigrette, 33
Chez Panisse, 46
Chicago, 9
Chicken: Chicken Wentletrap in the Thai Style, 65–66; Fruited Smoked Chicken and Chile Fettucine, 69–70; Green Grape/Yoghurt Chicken Spiedini, 75; Grilled Chicken/Wild Mushroom/Roasted Garlic Sandwich, 76
Chile-drying technique, 15
Chiles, 14, 26, 32, 54. See also Staples*: Chiles
Chiles, year-round: dried, 18; fresh, 18, 27, 35; seasonal, 18
Chinese donuts, 43
Chinese rice-flour bread, 43
Chinle, Arizona, 15
Chocolate. See Staples*: Chocolate

Chocolate Souffle Cake, 83
Chutney, 39
Cigars: Cohiba, Frisco, 85
Coffee: Cafe Fortissimo, 82–83. See also Staples*: Coffee
Cookie: Fennel Rice Cookies, 83–84
Corn: Orange-Buttermilk Corn Soup, 55
Coulis, 9
Couscous, 35
Cranberry (dried) Mustard, 41
Cream. See Staples*: Cream
Crème: fraîche, 47, 54; brûlée, 81; chantilly, 83
Crème Fraîche: Mountain Mousse with Lemon Crème Fraîche, 86
Crispy Noodle Nests with Tomatillos and Prawns, 66–67
Cucina povera, 46
Cucina ricca, 46
Cucumber Sambal Summer Soup, 54
Cuisine/Culture/Area: Asian, 13, 23, 33; Californian, 46; Chinese/Asian, 64; Creole, 13; Greek, 84; Hopi, 55; India(n), 54, 68; Indonesian, 33; Iranian, 84; Italian, 13, 38, 84; Mediterranean, 9, 11, 41, 48; Mexican Caribbean, 54; Mexican Native American, 28; Middle Eastern, 11, 41, 48; Native American, 11, 13, 15, 28, 55; North African, 11; North China Sea, 54; Oriental, 9, 44; Saudi Arabian Quarter (Bangkok), 66; Southeast Asian, 9, 11, 23, 40; Sicilian, 9, 56, 78; Thai, 13; Tropical, 33, 40; Turkish, 13
Cuoco, 78
Curry, 36
Curry (wet), 67–68
Czechoslovakians, 88

D

D'anjou pear, 86
Date: Date Mustard, 41; Utah Lamb, Pear, Date, and Toasted Bread Salad, 71; Date Onion Spread, 75
David, Elizabeth, 47
Des Essarts, 11
Desserts: Chapter 9, 80–90. See also "Beginnings or Endings: Sweet Dreams"

E

Eggplant: Roasted Eggplant Mozzarella Soup, 56–57
Eggs. See Staples*: Eggs

F

Family Home Evening, 73
Fennel: Fennel Rice Cookies, 83–84; Sweet Heater, 89
Fiery Sausage and Olive Soup, 54–55
Fig: Fig Mustard, 42; Fig Tapenade, 47
Filipino (pachero), 23
Fire/fire-spice stocks, 9. See also "Fruited Fire in the Kitchen"
Fisher, M. F. K., 21
Flour. See Staples*: Flour
Focaccia, 35, 73, 74
Fruit-based/fire-spice cooking, 9, 11
Fruit: groups, 17, 31; mustard, 37–44; seasons, 15–16, 31. See also Staples*: Fruits
"Fruited Fiery Broths: A Different Cooking Consideration" (Chapter 1), 12–19; How Fruit and Fire-Spice Stocks Evolved, 13–14; Varieties of Fruit and Fire-Spice Stocks, 14–15; Types of Fruit Stocks (basic, seasonal, variations), 15; Types of Fire-Spice and Fruit/Fire-Spice Stocks (basic, seasonal), 15; Fruit Seasons (fall/winter, spring, summer/fall), 16; Fruit Groups (bramble, bush, citron, pome, stone, vine, Mediterranean/ Tropical), 17; Year-Round Chiles (fresh, dried, seasonal), 18; Scoville Chile Pepper Heat Range, 19
"Fruited Fire in the Kitchen" (Chapter 2), 20–29; Basic Year-Round Fruit Stock, 22–23; Basic Year-Round Orange Stock, 23–24; Basic Year-Round Green Grape Stock, 24; Basic Year-Round Strawberry Stock, 24–25; Pureéd Fruit Stock, 25; Seasonal One-Fruit Stock, 25–26; Mediterranean- or Tropical-Fruit Stocks, 26; Multipurpose Fruited Broth, 26; Multipurpose Fruited Sauce, 26–27; Basic Year-Round Fire-Spice Stock, 27; Basic Year-Round Fruit/Fire-Spice Stock, 28; Seasonal

Fruit/Fire-Spice Stock, 28
Fruited Garlic Pasta with Walnuts, 68–69
Fruited Smoked Chicken and Chile Fettucine, 69–70
Fruited Vinaigrettes, 30–36. See also "Leeks, Limes, Lilies: Fruited Vinaigrettes"
Fruit-Fire Mustards, 39–44. See also "No Stranger to Sweat: Fruit-Fire Mustards"

G

Garam masala, 68
"Garden in a Pot: Soups and Stews" (Chapter 6), 52–59; Cucumber Sambal Summer Soup, 54; Fiery Sausage and Olive Soup, 54–55; Orange-Buttermilk Corn Soup, 55; Orange-Tomato Lamb Stew, 56; Roasted Eggplant Mozzarella Soup, 56–57; Scallop Celeriac Peanut Stew, 57; Sherried Shiitake Soup, 58; Singed Onion Soup, 51, 58; Tomatillo Tomato Tortilla Soup, 59
Garlic: Singed Garlic Chips, 48–49; Fruited Garlic Pasta with Walnuts, 68–69; Grilled Chicken/Wild Mushroom/Roasted Garlic Sandwich, 76. See also Staples*: Garlic
Garlic chips, 32, 43, 48, 70, 79
Gazpacho, 25
Ghee, 54, 68
Ginger: Pear Ginger Vinaigrette, 35; Singed Ginger Chips, 49. See also Staples*: Ginger
Gnocchi, 46
Grape (green): Basic Year-Round Green Grape Stock, 24; Green Grape/Yoghurt Chicken Spiedini, 75
Grappa, 90; syrup, moscato di, 82–83
Greek stiphado, 56
Green Grape/Yoghurt Chicken Spiedini, 75
Grilled Chicken/Wild Mushroom/Roasted Garlic Sandwich, 76
Grissini, 34
Guacamole Sandwich, 74
Guevara, Che, 46

H

Hayes Street Grill, 81
Hearts of Caesar Salad Sandwich with Roasted Orange Tomatoes, 76

Herbs. See Staples*: Herbs/Seeds
Hidden West (Utah), 9
"High-Peasant Eats: Appetizers" (Chapter 5), 45–51; Fig Tapenade, 47; Poet's Anchovy Toast, 47; Salsa Jacquelina, 48, 49; Singed Garlic Chips, 48–49; Singed Ginger Chips, 49; Singed Onions, 49; Smoked Trout Club Sandwich with Apple Horseradish, 50; Walnut Olive Rusks, 50–51; White Vegetable Broilcakes, 51
Holy Feast and Holy Fast (book), 53
Honey. See Staples*: Sugar/Honey
Horseradish root, 50
Hotevilla, Arizona, 15
Hungarians, 88

I

I Morti, 70
Ice cream, Canadian vanilla, 87
Il Primo Moture, 92
"Innocent Pleasures in the Hidden West" (Chapter 10), 92

J

Jam. See Staples*: Preserves
JazRanch, 9, 11, 13, 31, 83

K

Kiwi: Kiwi Mustard, 42
Kourambiedes, 46

L

La dolce vita, 81
Lamb: Orange-Tomato Lamb Stew, 56; Utah Lamb, Pear, Date, and Toasted Bread Salad, 71; Wasatch Mountain Meat Loaf, 79
Lavash, 33
Layered Pumpkin Mincemeat Pie, 84–85
"Leeks, Limes, Lilies: Fruited Vinaigrettes" (Chapter 3), 30–36; Apple or Dried Apple, 32; Apricot or Dried Apricot, 32; Cherry Radish, 33; Mango Chile, 33; Melon Chile, 34; Orange Sun-Dried Tomato, 34; Peach, 35; Pear Ginger, 35–36; Strawberry, 36
Lemon: Mountain Mousse with Lemon Crème Fraîche, 86. See also Staples*: Lemon
Lettuce. See Staples*: Lettuce

Lime: Avocado/Lime/Chile Sandwich, 74. See also Staples*: Lime

M

Mandarin orange, 24, 26
Mango Chile Vinaigrette, 33
Marinade, 11
Matzo crackers (egg/onion), 41, 51
Meals, Solitary: Chapter 8, 72–79. See also "Sneakers and Gewürztraminer: Solitary Meals"
Meat. See Staples*: Meat
Mediterranean fruit stock, 26
Medjhool date, 71
Melon Chile Vinaigrette, 34
Meneghina alla griglia, 81
Milano, Italy, 81
Milk: Sleeping Milk Compote Cake, 88. See also Staples*: Milk
Milton, John, 38
Mincemeat: Layered Pumpkin Mincemeat Pie, 84–85
Mormon, 11, 73
Mostarda di frutta, 38, 39
Mousse: Mountain Mousse with Lemon Crème Fraîche, 86
Mozzarella: Roasted Eggplant Mozzarella Soup, 56–57
Muscovado: Pear and Muscovado Sugar Cake, 86–87
Mushroom, 14–15; Sherried Shiitake Soup, 58; Grilled Chicken/Wild Mushroom/Roasted Garlic Sandwich, 76
Mustards, Fruit-Fire: Chapter 4, 37–44. See also "No Stranger to Sweat: Fruit-Fire Mustards"; Staples*: Mustard (prepared)

N

Naan, 54, 68
Nana Restaurant, 66
Napa Valley grappa, 43
Nignon, Edouard, 13
"No Stranger to Sweat: Fruit-Fire Mustards" (Chapter 4), 37–44; Italian Fruit Mustard (Mostarda di frutta), 39; Apple, 40; Banana, 40; Cranberry (dried), 41; Date, 41; Fig (dried), 42; Kiwi, 42; Orange, 43; Papaya (green), 43; Plum, 44; Raspberry, 44

Noodles: Crispy Noodle Nests with Tomatillos and Prawns, 66–67
Nutella, 90
Nuts. See Staples*: Nuts

O

Oaxacan, 59
Oils. See Staples*: Oils
Olive paste, 47
Olive: Walnut Olive Rusks, 50; Fiery Sausage and Olive Soup, 54
Onion: Singed Onion Soup, 58; Date Onion Spread, 75. See also Staples*: Olives
Onions. See Staples*: Onions
Oquirrh range, 79
Orange, 14–15; Orange Stock, 23–24, 26, 27, 28, 54, 55; Orange Sun-Dried Tomato Vinaigrette, 34; Orange Mustard, 41; Orange Buttermilk Corn Soup, 55; Orange Tomato Lamb Stew, 56; Hearts of Caesar Salad Sandwich with Roasted Orange Tomatoes, 76–77. See also Staples*: Orange
Oriental Hotel (Bangkok), 66
Orvieto, Italy, 81
Orzo, 43

P

Pachero, 23
Pacific Bay Baking, 50
Pain au levain, 77
Palagonia, Sicily, 41
Pancetta, 34
Papaya Mustard, 43
Paradise Regained, 38
Parks, Tim, 81
"Pas D'Action," 22
Pasta: Fruited Garlic Pasta with Walnuts, 68–69; Fruited Smoked Chicken and Chile Fettucine, 69–70; San Giuseppe Pasta Con Sarde, 78. See also Staples*: Pasta
Pasta puttanesca, 46
Pasticcerias, 81
Pastina, 35, 43
Paz, Octavio, 92
Peanut: Scallop Celeriac Peanut Stew, 57
Peach Vinaigrette, 35
Pear: Pear Ginger Vinaigrette, 35–36; Utah Lamb, Pear, Date, and Toasted Bread Salad, 71; Pear and Muscovado Sugar Cake, 86–87
Pear eau de vie, 87
Peasant food (appetizers), 46–51. See also "High Peasant Eats: Appetizers"

Pepperidge Farm.
  See Staples*: Bread.
Perciatelli, 78
Perfume (book), 39
Pernod, 51
Pesto, 11
Philosophy, cooking, 9
Pie: Layered Pumpkin
  Mincemeat Pie, 84–85
Pineapple Brownie, 87
Pizza, singed onions
  with, 49
Pizza furioso, 46
Pizzette, 70, 77–78;
Pizzette D'Amici, 70
Plum Mustard, 44
Poet's Anchovy Toast,
  47
Pork, 44
Prawns: Crispy Noodle
  Nests with Tomatillos
  and Prawns, 66–67
Preserves. See Staples*:
  Preserves
Pretzel, 40
Prosciutto, 34
Pudding: Banana Rice
  Pudding, 82
Pumpkin: Layered
  Pumpkin Mincemeat
  Pie, 84–85

R
Raspberry Mustard, 44
Relish, 39
Restorantes, 53
Restoratives, 53
Rice: Black Jaz Scallops
  with Black Sweet Rice,
  64; Risotto Pizzette,
  77–78; Banana Rice
  Pudding, 82; Fennel
  Rice Cookies, 83.
  See also Staples*: Rice
Rice flour, 83
Ricotta, 38
Riley, David, 46
Risotto, 77–78
Risotto Pizzette, 77–78
Roasted Eggplant
  Mozzarella Soup,
  56–57
Rocket, 53
Rogenbrot, 76
Rose flower water, 83

S
Salad: Utah Lamb, Pear,
  Date, and Toasted
  Bread Salad, 71;
  Hearts of Caesar Salad
  Sandwich with Roasted
  Orange Tomatoes,
  76–77
Salsa Jacquelina, 48, 59
Salt Lake City, Utah, 9,
  83
San Francisco, 31, 81
San Giuseppe Pasta
  Con Sarde, 78
San Juan Capistrano, 9
Sandwiches: Chapter 8,
  72–79. See also
  "Sneakers and
  Gewürztraminer:
  Solitary Meals"
Sauces, 9, 11, 13;
  fruited, 26–27

Sausage: chicken, 42;
  and fennel patties, 53;
  Italian, sweet, 54; Fiery
  Sausage and Olive
  Soup, 54–55
Scallops: Scallop
  Celeriac Peanut Stew,
  57; Black Jaz Scallops
  with Black Sweet Rice,
  64
Scoville Chile Pepper
  Heat Range, 19, 21
Seasonal fruit stock,
  25–26
Seasoning (liquid). See
  Staples*: Seasoning
  (liquid)
Sebastopol apple juice,
  50
Seeds. See Staples*:
  Herbs/Seeds
Seafood. See Staples*:
  Seafood
Sherried Shiitake Soup,
  58
Shiitake mushrooms,
  58, 76
Shrimp, steamed, 43
Singed: Garlic Chips,
  49; Onions, 49; Onion
  Soup, 58
Singed onion oil, 58
The Sleeping Beauty, 22
Sleeping Milk Compote
  Cake, 88
Slop of Joe's, 56
Smoked Trout Club
  Sandwich with Apple
  Horseradish, 50
"Sneakers and
  Gewürztraminer:
  Solitary Meals"
  (chapter 8), 72–79;
  Avocado/Lime/Chile
  Sandwich (Guacamole
  Sandwich), 74;
  Cauliflower Stracinati,
  74; Date Onion
  Spread, 75; Green
  Grape/Yoghurt
  Chicken Spiedini, 75;
  Grilled Chicken/Wild
  Mushroom/Roasted
  Garlic Sandwich, 76;
  Hearts of Caesar Salad
  Sandwich with
  Roasted Orange
  Tomatoes, 76–77;
  Risotto Pizzette,
  77–78; San Giuseppe
  Pasta Con Sarde, 78;
  Wasatch Mountain
  Meat Loaf, 79
Socratic moderation, 29
Soups, 13, 33, 49, 51.
  See also "Garden in a
  Pot: Soups and Stews"
Spices. See Staples*:
  Spices
Spiedini, 75
Spirits. See Staples*:
  Wines/Beers/Spirits
Spiritual connection, 9
St. Joseph's Day, 9, 78
Starbucks, 81
Stews, 23, 51, 71.
  See also "Garden in a
  Pot: Soups and Stews"
Stiphado: Greek,
  Sicilian, 56

Stocks: fruit (basic/
  seasonal/variations),
  12–19, 20–29;
  fruit/fire-spice, 12–19,
  20–29; meat-based:
  11, 13; mother, 13,
  12–19, 20–29. See
  also "Fruited Fire in
  the Kitchen"
Stracinati, 74
Strand, Mark, 73
Strawberry: Strawberry
  Stock, 24–25;
  Strawberry Vinaigrette,
  36
Sugar. See Staples*:
  Sugar/Honey
Summary: Chapter 10,
  92
Suppers: Chapter 7,
  60–71. See also
  "Tongue Touchers:
  Enraged Suppers and
  Otherwise"
Suskind, Patrick
  (author), 39
Sweet Black Rice, 64
Sweet Heater, 89
Sweets, 80–90. See also
  "Beginnings or
  Endings: Sweet
  Dreams"
Syrups, 9; fruit, 47, 49;
  moscato di grappa,
  82–83; Sweet Heater,
  89; light corn, 89

T
Tagliatelle, 68
Tarocco orange, 41
Tchaikovsky, 22
Tecate, 32
Tesuque, New Mexico,
  49
Thai: Chicken
  Wentletrap in the Thai
  Style, 65–66
Tomatillo: Crispy
  Noodle Nests with
  Tomatillos and
  Prawns, 66–67;
  Tomatillo Tomato Tortilla
  Soup, 59
Tomato, 14–15;
  Orange-Tomato Lamb
  Stew, 56; Tomatillo
  Tomato Tortilla Soup,
  59; Hearts of Caesar
  Salad Sandwich with
  Roasted Orange
  Tomatoes, 76–77.
  See also Staples*:
  Tomato
"Tongue Touchers:
  Enraged Suppers and
  Otherwise" (Chapter
  7), 60–71; Black Jaz
  Pickling Potion, 62;
  Shortened Black Jaz,
  63; Black Jaz Scallops
  with Black Sweet Rice,
  64; Chicken
  Wentletrap in the Thai
  Style, 65–66; Crispy
  Noodle Nests with
  Tomatillos and
  Prawns, 66–67; Curry
  (wet), 67–68; Fruited
  Garlic Pasta with
  Walnuts, 68–69;

Fruited Smoked
  Chicken and Chile
  Fettucine, 69–70;
  Pizzette D'Amici, 70;
  Utah Lamb, Pear,
  Date, and Toasted
  Bread Salad, 71
Torn, Rip, 9
Tortilla: Tomatillo
  Tomato Tortilla Soup,
  59
Tortoni Jacquelina, 90
Tropical dishes, 40
Tropical fruit stock, 26
Trout, smoked, 35, 50
Tuba City, Arizona, 15

U
Uintahs, high, 86
Utah, 9, 11, 83
Utah Lamb, Pear, Date,
  and Toasted Bread
  Salad, 71

V
Vancouver, British
  Columbia, 64
Vegetables. See Staples*:
  Vegetables
Vernor's Ginger Ale, 40
Vicari, Sicily, 41
Victoria, British
  Columbia, 64
Vinaigrettes: Chapter 3,
  30–36. See also
  "Leeks, Limes, Lilies:
  Fruited Vinaigrettes"
Vinegar. See Staples*:
  Vinegar
Vitamin chile heat, 61

W
Walnut: Walnut Olive
  Rusks, 50; Fruited
  Garlic Pasta with
  Walnuts, 68–69
Wasatch Mountain Meat
  Loaf, 79
Water: orange, rose
  flower, 83
Waters, Alice, 46
West, Mae, 31
Wet seasoning, 31
The Whole Chile Pepper
  Book, 29
White Vegetable
  Broilcakes, 51
Wines/Beers/Spirits.
  See Staples*:
  Wines/Beers/Spirits
WoodyAllenesque style,
  14

Y
Yin and yang, 9
Yoghurt: Green
  Grape/Yoghurt
  Chicken Spiedini, 75

Z
Zwieback, 33, 51, 82